Live Like WES

Home Decor Inspired by Wes Anderson Movies

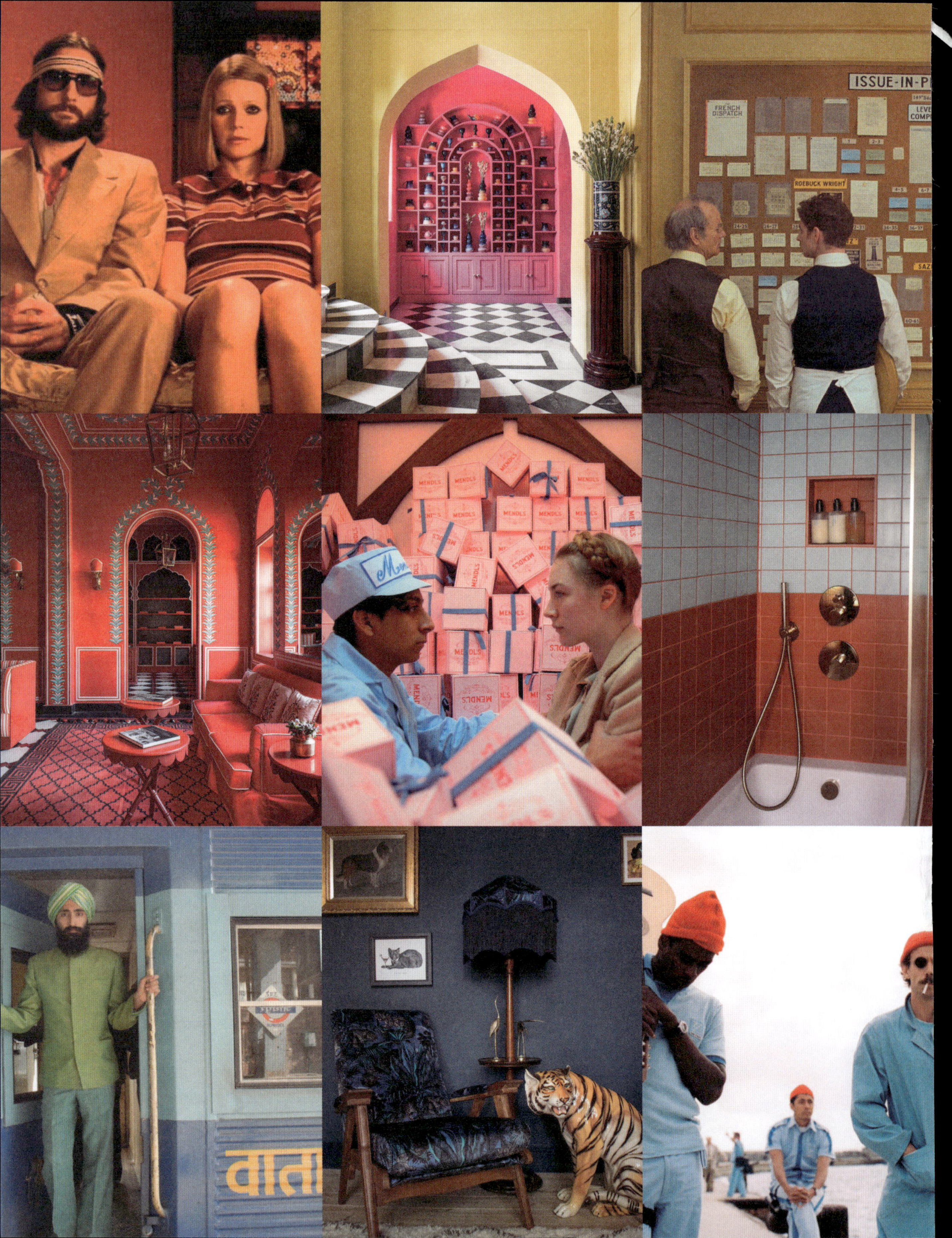
ISSUE-IN-P
FRENCH DISPATCH
ROEBUCK WRIGHT
MENDLS

Live Like WES

Home Decor Inspired by Wes Anderson Movies

JESSIE ATKINSON

Unofficial and unauthorized

ollow the Yellow Brick Road

WELCOME TO THE WORLD OF WES
6
TOP TEN WES-STYLE INTERIOR TIPS
11
COLOUR LIKE WES
12
IT'S ALL IN THE DETAIL
14
SEVEN SECOND-HAND SHOPPING TIPS
17

Bohemian Kitsch in the Living Room
INSPIRED BY *THE ROYAL TENENBAUMS* 18

Cottagecore in the Kitchen
INSPIRED BY *FANTASTIC MR. FOX* 42

Rajasthani Deco in the Hallways
INSPIRED BY *THE DARJEELING LIMITED* 66

European Charm in the Office
INSPIRED BY *THE FRENCH DISPATCH* 88

Whimsy in the Nooks and Crannies
INSPIRED BY *MOONRISE KINGDOM* 110

1950s Americana in the Dining Room
INSPIRED BY *ASTEROID CITY* 136

Nautical Mediterranean in the Bathroom
INSPIRED BY *THE LIFE AQUATIC* 158

Dopamine Decor in the Bedroom
INSPIRED BY *THE GRAND BUDAPEST HOTEL* 180

INDEX
204
ACKNOWLEDGEMENTS
207

Welcome to the World of WES

Wesley Wales Anderson was born in 1969. His first short film, *Bottle Rocket*, came into the world in 1993, followed three years later by his first feature length of the same name. Most agree that his signature aesthetic style was birthed with *The Royal Tenenbaums*, which played in cinemas in 2001. Since then, his exacting and instantly recognizable brand of paintbox brights, symmetry and whimsy has made 'Wes Anderson' shorthand for all things kitsch, fanciful and, above all, beautiful.

We've all seen the Accidentally Wes Anderson trend inspired by the films and the book that followed: folks finding themselves in sets and situations that have the signature 'Wes' look. But what if you want to live like Wes Anderson on *purpose*? Some will feel that way about other creations, of course: Marvel, *Star Wars*, the canon of David Lynch…the difference with an Anderson production is that it is actually conceivable to recreate. There's no CGI here, nor so much surrealism that an associated project becomes impossible. Instead, everything you see in the frame of an American Empirical film has been lovingly handmade by crews and craftspeople that total in the hundreds.

If you have emerged from an experience with one of these films feeling the urge to immerse yourself in that world for longer, this book aims to help you do so, by putting very un-accidental techniques into practice in order to curate an aesthetic that brings you closer to this great director's work. Though I'll give cocktail recipes, dinner party ideas and playlists around eight movies in the pages that follow, *Live Like Wes* primarily does this through the medium of interior design.

Anderson's films' effect on the world of decor cannot be overstated. Once, it might have been called 'jazzy', 'eccentric' or 'esoteric' to paint your walls bubblegum-pink and hang pictures of cartoons alongside records and ornate-framed paintings; or considered tacky to display ornaments or buy lighting intended for children. But in Wes Anderson's – and now his fans' – hands, these old definitions of kitsch have been reframed in favour of something more purposeful and less self-conscious. Today, and in part thanks to Anderson and team's careful curation, homes that go down these paths have never been more desirable.

It started, as I've already suggested, with *The Royal Tenenbaums*. Sure, care of setting was there

ABOVE Childhood whimsy and opulence combine in the sharing of chocolate cake and milk under a crystal chandelier in *The Royal Tenenbaums*.

in *Bottle Rocket* and 1998's *Rushmore*, but most will agree that the saturated, hyper-stylized spaces that would become Anderson's signature first blossomed in the Hamilton Heights red-brick mansion inhabited by the Tenenbaum family. An enormous cross-section of a dollhouse-like boat followed in *The Life Aquatic* in 2004. By 2007 and *The Darjeeling Limited* that picture-book Andersonian style had become as inevitable as a cast of off-kilter characters that included Owen Wilson, a melancholy undertone and a love of analogue.

ABOVE On the set of *Asteroid City*, in which a farm between Spain's Chinchón and Colmenar de Oreja stands in for the American desert.

With 2009 and *Fantastic Mr. Fox*, Anderson hit upon the format that is arguably his best: by pivoting to animation and puppetry, he was more thoroughly able to exercise his own personal brand of perfectionism. In this world, everything from a fox teenager's bedroom to a supermarket aisle could be perfected in miniature. While he had actors including George Clooney (as Mr Fox) and Meryl Streep (as Mrs Fox) record their lines while running about the countryside (in order to avoid the stuffiness of a studio voiceover), the puppet 'actors' could be placed just so in the frame, becoming as stylized as the tree home and flint mines that surrounded them.

It was a film that Anderson seemed to take with him into his future projects: *Moonrise Kingdom* was more fantastical, *The Grand Budapest Hotel* more beautiful, *The French Dispatch* more organized and *Asteroid City* more cartoonish than anything that had gone before. Each showed such a precise sense of stylization that it's almost inconceivable that they too were not moved by hand across a tiny stage. (That did happen again, of course, in *Isle of Dogs*, which doesn't have its own chapter in this book for lack of specific interior design inspiration.)

Through it all, Anderson's all-encompassing love of beauty and perfection (in design, if not always in storyline) shines most prominently in the sets that he commissions for his narratives: in the walls, the ceilings, the floors and everything contained within them. It is in these surroundings – as well as through characteristic blocking and *mise en scène* – that Wes Anderson has cultivated a following that goes beyond cinematic interest, touching something more akin to spiritual wonder and an aesthetic playbook for living a charmed life.

Here you'll find my own translation of this playbook, varying from how to decorate your home to themed dinner parties and DIY projects inspired by the films. The book covers eight of Wes's most distinctive films, each of which I have paired with a room in the home as well as an interior design style. The practice turned out to be surprisingly intuitive: *The Royal Tenenbaums* has the essence of a bohemian kitsch living room; *Moonrise Kingdom*, a whimsical alcove; *Fantastic Mr. Fox*, a cottagecore kitchen, and so on. Almost no discipline or niche goes untouched by the paintbrush of Wes and his band of artisans, which has done more than give fans practical ideas on how to add a touch of magic into their spaces; it has somewhat demystified interior design.

In the writing of this book, I have watched and rewatched Anderson's films more than anyone – even a fan like me – ever reasonably should.

Probably Anderson will not have expected anyone to have watched them as much, or as closely, as I have. And yet such fixed attention has not revealed clangers or dangling threads. On the contrary, it has confirmed Anderson's perfectionism on an even more detailed scale. The minutest of details, from the badges on the *Moonrise Kingdom* Khaki Scouts' uniforms to the straw dispenser on the counter of the *Asteroid City* Luncheonette, hold up to the closest scrutiny. Equally, every minor on-screen prop, painting and piece of furniture lends itself to fruitful inspiration to apply to your home and life, whether it be in a big project or a tiny tweak (you will find ideas for both in the chapters that follow).

This project has cultivated in me an even greater admiration for Anderson and his team, most notably production designer Adam Stockhausen, who undertook the role for *Moonrise Kingdom*, *The Grand Budapest Hotel*, *Isle of Dogs*, *The French Dispatch*, *Asteroid City*, four Roald Dahl shorts that included *The Wonderful Story of Henry Sugar*, and 2025's *The Phoenician Scheme*. Working with Wes, Stockhausen has been responsible for many of the wonders that form the basis for the inspirations in this book.

Each film has a long list of specialists within the art and speciality departments around Anderson and Stockhausen. The next time you watch one of these films, I encourage you to read the credits, which reveal some of that expertise. For example, *The Grand Budapest Hotel* had a Klimt forger on the books, while *Asteroid City* required both a yodelling consultant and a lasso consultant.

Paying close attention to these peoples's work has shown me how lovingly anything can be made if you have the will to pay proper attention. It has shown me that you can go further than just admire something; you can bring some of that joy into your own life, whether it be redecorating your sofa, making a gallery wall of your kitchen magnets, or putting faux thatch on to the inside of your kitchen ceiling. It has made me more enthusiastic than ever before about the idea of putting effort into making a tablescape that evokes the dining car of *The Darjeeling Limited* and then serving a meal inspired by the food in the film. It has even made me pay closer attention to my own life, both in work and out, to imitate some of that beautiful perfectionism that Wes Anderson's projects thrive on.

If you're reading this book, I already know that you feel the same way about Wes Anderson's films. What I hope is that it brings you some practical tips, new ideas and fun projects on how to eat, drink and decorate – how to Live Like Wes.

Jessie Atkinson, 2025

LEFT Anderson's exacting direction is arguably best suited to the puppetry on display in 2009's *Fantastic Mr. Fox*.

Top Ten Wes-style Interior TIPS

1. Study your colour wheels
Dedicated fans will be able to spot an Anderson film from its palette alone. Let this boldness with colour be your inspiration, drenching skirting to ceiling in bright or whimsical hues, and experimenting with combinations such as red and pink (as seen in *The Royal Tenenbaums*) or blue and yellow (*Asteroid City*).

2. Get in line
Symmetry is another prominent feature in the Anderson playbook. Use it to satisfying effect with matching ornaments on mantels, twin lamps, bookends placed just so and framed pictures hung with spirit levels.

3. Something old, nothing new
Most of Anderson's films are set in the mid-20th century with reverent use of period props. To properly create a *Moonrise Kingdom* environment, then, make a habit of flea markets and antiques shops.

4. Hide your tech
Anderson is no Luddite, but if something can be done with practical effects and in analogue, it will be. Conceal television screens behind colourful shutters when not in use, favour record players over stereos, and don't let your e-reader stop you from filling your shelves with books.

5. Embrace the peculiar
From Ash's model train set in *Fantastic Mr. Fox* to Chas's rotating tie display in *The Royal Tenenbaums*, there are oddities at every turn in the homes of Anderson's characters, giving you free rein to buck conservatism in favour of the strange and beautiful.

6. Make it maximal
This is no book for the minimally minded; for an Anderson home, maximalism is the order of the day. That doesn't mean clutter, but it does mean go big and bold with colours, patterns and themes, and don't be afraid to fill your home with beautiful objects that make you smile.

7. Draw exciting contrasts
One way to master interior design is to become adroit at the intriguing contrast. That can certainly mean a blue and a red in tandem, but it also entails experimentation with texture, such as a straw rug on a stone floor, or with theme, such as a modern print in an antique frame.

8. The handmade has it
Anderson's productions are full of props and ephemera created by brilliant craftspeople. Embrace the wonder of skill with pieces picked up from experts in their craft.

9. Curate your collection
Roman Coppola didn't build a Wes Anderson production in a day. Treat your Anderson-inspired home like a curated museum collection and add to it over time.

10. Rely on what you love
Anderson's films gained popularity because they favour childlike whimsy and off-kilter choices over stiff, rigid rules. The ultimate Anderson move, then, is to rely on the things that bring you joy.

Colour Like WES

Wes Anderson has been known to work with black and white, but his films are overwhelmingly preoccupied with brilliant, eye-popping colours. This is one of the reasons people love his films; only a dedicated ascetic could resist the candy-store hues exhibited in scene after scene.

It's true that saturation is dialled up in post-production, but even if it weren't, the slicks of paint slung by Anderson's army of artists would still make these films some of the brightest in movie history. The visual identity derived from this knack with vibrancy is self-evident. It is an aesthetic that has made Anderson one of the most recognizable filmmakers; it is also a large part of what we can learn from this cinematic painter.

PICK A CONTRAST COLOUR

Most of Anderson's films have a strong colour identity (think of *The Grand Budapest Hotel* and you will inevitably think in pink). Look again, however, and you will also discover an exciting supporting cast of contrasting and complementary colours. A living room painted all in pink is a bold move indebted to *The Grand Budapest Hotel* and *The Royal Tenenbaums* – especially when the skirting boards, radiators and perhaps even ceiling are painted in the same hue. Remember, though, to bring in some tonality or contrast. In M. Gustave's world of hospitality, it comes through in red carpets, purple uniforms and green palms, while in the Tenenbaums' mansion pink is instead delicately cut through with various tones of red, from vermilion to crimson.

The pattern continues throughout Anderson's filmography. Yellow looks sumptuous in *The Darjeeling Limited* offset with zingy orange and deep blue. In *Asteroid City*, turquoise is used in conjunction with dusty mesa-yellow and dark cactus-green. Look for surprising combinations in your own interior colour palettes to elevate the look.

STICK WITH A THEME

From Anderson's characters' costumes to their homes and the towns they inhabit, colour themes are carried seamlessly throughout Anderson films, from the orange-bathed English countryside of *Fantastic Mr. Fox* to the Mediterranean seas of *The Life Aquatic* awash with blue.

Likewise, in your home colour can have a cohesive effect, creating a sense of flow throughout and maximizing the feeling of space. You don't have to paint every room the same shade, but consider how the colours you use in each room work together and flow from one space to the next. You can also use colours from one room in a different way in another. For example, the main colour in the living room could be an accent in the hallway or picked out in the soft furnishings of the kitchen/dining area.

SAY GOODBYE TO GREY

This is not a book about colour, but the topic naturally permeates every discussion of an Anderson film. One of the easiest ways to bring a little Wes Anderson magic into your home, then, is to wave goodbye to beige and neutral tones, and embrace rich jewel tones, sorbet brights and paint-box primaries. One of the most important things to rethink before you dive in is your relationship with which colours you consider appropriate in a home. You may have felt chained to the greys and creams of modern-day design before, but from now on let's take the cue of Margot Tenenbaum, Mrs Fox, Suzy Bishop and M. Gustave.

OPPOSITE LEFT The distinctive stripes of Colours of Arley come in every hue, from teal-green to baby blue, bubblegum-pink to acid yellow.

—

OPPOSITE RIGHT YesColours! gives Wes-style inspiration with this bold bedroom with walls in Joyful Pink. Green tones are a masterclass in the Anderson art of contrast.

It's all in the DETAIL

A space is instantly recognizable by its whole – the way a sofa looks beside a lamp, the effect of a curtain in a window – but most of the tips to follow in this book are concerned with what truly makes a home something personal: the finer details. It is kismet that interior design can be at its most accessible and affordable in the details, because it is exactly this – details – on which Wes Anderson's films, and therefore his aesthetic, operate.

Loving dedication to craft and to doing things the proper way is what goes into the *Asteroid City* vending machines, *Darjeeling Limited* tea sets, *Isle of Dogs* puppets, and so on, in Anderson's universe. It is also the secret sauce poured into any room with the aim of provoking wonder and joy. Whether you're investing in a new sofa and curtains or not, the real opportunity presents itself in smaller tweaks: a new pair of zany cushions and a contrasting throw can make an old couch bohemian kitsch, while your existing curtains could find a new, more interesting life in front of an alcove or around a bed.

Expense spared or not, the real magic of an eccentric home is in its smallest quirks. How many people would love a home with a single stained-glass window or an errant pillar? This book aims to inspire you to introduce these kinds of follies yourself, whether it be through a riotous peel-and-stick tile splashback or a towering stack of books in the corner of the hallway.

You may even find that the tiniest of details make up the desired visual and emotional identity of your home, whether they're immediately obvious or not. The completed fantasy books owned by Suzy Bishop in *Moonrise Kingdom* aren't visible in their entirety, but the viewer's trust in these books' existence is what brings magic to the screen, just as an engraved cutlery set will bring magic to even a closed kitchen drawer.

ANDERSONVILLE

Seven second-hand shopping TIPS

To achieve Anderson-level attention to detail and craft, you will need to invest time and care. A single trip to Ikea won't deliver the goods on this one, so instead make a habit of shopping second-hand, riffling through charity shops and vintage stores, and frequenting car-boot sales and flea markets.

1. Find reputable shops
The first thing you're going to want is a list of spots that carry the kind of things you love. Your own personal taste is what matters most in the creation of a home inspired by Wes Anderson, but if you want to follow his excellent precedent, look for mid-century modern shops.

2. Take it to the market, both on and offline
You can find special items in places beyond your city's dedicated antiques shops. Look for mid-century modern furniture and kitsch doodads in flea markets, yard sales, second-hand stores, car-boot sales and online marketplaces. You can also often find smaller interior design pieces in vintage shops that are largely dedicated to selling clothes.

3. Make visits a habit
Like shopping for vintage clothing, you probably won't find something you love on the first try. Instead, you'll need to make semi-regular visits to the shops and online spaces that best match your taste. With dedication and careful perusal, you'll soon find the exact things you've been hoping for.

4. Shop on holiday
Don't just search in your home town; if you're away from your locality, poke your head into antiques shops and flea markets. You may find a hidden treasure made even more special by the memories it will carry.

5. Ask store owners for advice
Most furniture and antiques shops will be owned by someone who acquires their stock themselves, meaning they should know a lot about each piece. They might also be able to help you source something specific that you've been seeking.

6. Don't just shop for furniture
Vintage emporiums are often filled with minute trinkets, the likes of which will make up the complete picture of your newly Wes-ified home. Look for ceramics, crockery, frames, books, ornaments, and even jewellery and scarves that can be repurposed as light pulls or doilies.

7. Upcycle
Some mid-century furniture can look a touch dilapidated, but with a little sanding, varnishing and a new set of feet or knobs, you can make it look exactly as you'd hoped, with the added benefit of personalization.

OPPOSITE This living room by Hollis Loudon delights in detail, from the prints on the assorted cushions to the teapot on the coffee table.

Bohemian Kitsch

The ROYAL TENENBAUMS

THE LIVING ROOM

Part 1

Wealthy people have been decorating their homes in an eccentric manner since time immemorial. During the Victorian era painter Frederic Leighton saw fit to commission a mosaic-tiled fountain room for his west London abode. In the late 19th century, over in the USA, heiress Sarah Winchester used the fortune she had inherited from her dead husband's arms company to create a Gothic mansion full of maze-like corridors and stairs leading nowhere. So it is with the titular family in *The Royal Tenenbaums* and their multi-storey townhouse, which is a collage of styles representative of each family member, as well as every Wes Anderson fan's favourite thing: a monument to kitsch.

A KALEIDOSCOPE OF KITSCH

While Anderson's third feature film is as much tragedy as it is comedy, the interior design of the Tenenbaum house is decidedly more stable – and delightfully lived-in. With interesting patterns abounding on wallpaper and carpets, bright paints melding with vintage lighting, and brass abutting wood, it's a true shrine to maximalist idiosyncrasies. The best part of all this is that you needn't own a listed mansion to create your own temple to trashy; with some well-placed ornaments and savvy design choices, you can bring this eclectic, homely vibe straight into your living room.

PREVIOUS PAGES Vermilion walls, Tiffany-esque glass mosaics, a chintzy gold sofa… the Tenenbaum mansion is a museum of kitsch.

—

BELOW Margot Tenenbaum's room is furnished with Scalamandré wallpaper and tribal masks in a maximalist mash-up only Anderson could dream up.

COLOUR PALETTE WARM RETRO

Where *The Royal Tenenbaums* mansion flourishes as a tapestry of home life is in the details. In this house, kitsch doesn't mean an ironic love of the tacky and ugly, but a sincere investment in individuality that transforms what some might consider tacky and ugly into something charming and homely.

In Margot's room, bright red Scalamandré zebra-print wallpaper runs throughout, transcending door jambs and finding its way into her en suite as an explicit reference to the animal character she portrays in her first play. For Richie, a zigzag of bright green and blue carpet nods to the balls and summer sky of a tennis match without being too on-the-nose in colour. More Wall Street than Wes, Chas's room is still very much part of his family's style, whether he wants it that way or not; his hand-drawn exercise diagrams take pride of place like his brother's portraits of Margot, and the maze of bright yellow mouse tunnels is eccentrically incongruous to the rest of the working space. The result is a rich palette of rust-reds, golden yellows and warm browns, punctuated by pops of blue and turquoise in Anderson's signature retro style.

BELOW Offset rich reds with accents in cooler shades, such as the teal of the lampshade on this beautifully curated bar trolley by Hollis Loudon.

LEFT Note Margot Tenenbaum's library of plays, featuring works by Harold Pinter, Arthur Miller and Anton Chekhov, among others.

—

OPPOSITE Ben Stiller's Chas Tenenbaum is a contemporary contrast to the 19th-century set in 1990s Adidas.

THE SPACES OF GENIUS CHILDREN

Royal and Etheline's gifted Family of Geniuses inhabit their own enormous rooms, each of which is large enough to qualify as a living area as much as somewhere to sleep. The size and detail of these spaces aren't only a symptom of wealth that means the siblings needn't share a space, but also an indicator of liberalism that allows individuality to flourish. (It also means they're lonely, but let's set that aside for the purposes of this book!) Anderson and team's vision of each room read like dream playgrounds to pastime. Characteristically of Wes's fascination with childhood, we never see the adults' bedroom, with focus instead remaining on the children's rooms, all of which remain unchanged into their thirties.

It could be a worse case of arrested development, however. Margot's room has a ballet barre, a miniature library of plays, a typewriter and an en suite that moonlights as a darkroom. Chas's space is more office than anything else, with rows of identical grey books on beige shelving that matches his PC and Bakelite rotary phone. There's also a punchbag, presumably for when the pressures of being a ten-year-old financial entrepreneur get too much. In Richie's room, tennis is the main focus, although there is also a drum kit and a mini science lab, plus sweet childlike pictures painted on to the walls.

Simply put, these three rooms function as distinct living spaces: as different as the siblings, united only by their wooden doors and crystal chandeliers. And it is this individuality that we can take into our own homes.

ORIGINAL FEATURES

If you're lucky enough to live in a home that bears its original markings, you're in a fortunate minority alongside the Tenenbaums, who live in a huge red-brick mansion in New York's Hamilton Heights. Boasting 50 windows, hardwood parquet flooring throughout and six fireplaces, the real-life building was originally inhabited by Charles H Tuttle – the Republican nominee who ran against FDR in 1930. He lost, but in a home like this, who can say if he was even that sad about it.

It's no surprise that the 550-m^2 19th-century property was going for a huge $20,000 pcm in rent back in 2021. Part of that cost is owed to the period features that still abound, and which can be clearly seen in the 2001 film. There are stained-glass windows and sliding wood doors, curved oak staircases, and a turret. Note that the listing photos from 2021 prove once and for all why wholesale renovations are a bad idea…the hyper-modernized kitchen and main bathroom are totally at odds with the rest of the house. Perhaps that's why we don't see these spaces in *The Royal Tenenbaums* at all.

ODE TO THE PAST

Everything about the Tenenbaum mansion is nostalgic, such as the period detailing, which calls back to a traditional era before the 1970s in which the film is set. In a more literal sense, the childrens's unchanged bedrooms are proof of the family's inability to move beyond their youth, with everything up to and including Chas's rotating tie display untouched as the relic of a long past childhood. When a 30-something Richie sets up in a tent in the ballroom so that his dad can use his room, he probably isn't aware of just how much he's yearning to return to that time when he camped under a bench at the museum with Margot.

This chronic nostalgia chimes with themes beyond the aesthetic. Mother Etheline's career is in archaeology, meaning that she spends her days excavating the bones of people who lived in times gone by. Having her family all under one roof again is clearly an extension of this fascination with the past; she toys with the idea of getting back with her selfish, estranged husband and installs her children in bedrooms that haven't seen so much as a lick of paint in the two decades since we see them as kids. There's no need for you to be quite so regressive – or literal – in your own home. Instead, kitsch should portray a comfortable and welcoming environment that's easy to introduce with some clever tricks involving contrast, colour and curios.

BELOW As an archaeologist, Etheline Tenenbaum's reliance on the past extends well beyond her interior design tastes.

—

OPPOSITE Wellie the Westie is a rare neutral in Phaedra Brown's warm and welcoming home in Maryland, USA.

BRING THE ROYAL TENENBAUMS HOME

PLANT
Money trees, string of buttons or elephant bush

LIGHT FITTING
Crystal chandeliers

COLOUR COMBO
Pink with red

SMALL TWEAKS
Frame homemade paintings; add unexpected colour; thrift for eccentric ornaments; make a kitchen magnet 'gallery wall'; line up existing lamps symmetrically

BIG PROJECTS
Colour drench ceilings and walls; embrace a theme; buy up oak, brass and chintzy furniture.

BRING OUT YOUR INNER CHILD

We don't get the opportunity to read any of Etheline's *Family of Geniuses*, but since it's written by a bohemian parent of the 1970s, we can presume that it features a chapter about embracing play. What other kind of parent would leave the decoration of their rooms entirely up to the child? You might not want to mine your own children's creativity for interior advice, but you could interrogate your own inner child. If bright green carpet would have been your choice at age eight, some clever decisions for the rest of your lounge – a calmer, tonal painted wall – will make the resulting space look more Tenenbaum than terrible twos. You could even introduce props that represent your childhood hobbies: hanging on the wall, stacked on the bookcase, as a pattern on the rugs. Your options can start as small as hanging a framed print of your favourite childhood book to the wall or displaying your high-school hockey stick.

For something simpler, you could do a Richie and make a gallery wall of your or your kids' paintings. Adding frames and creating an organized spread will immediately elevate the practice from something scrappy, hastily taped to the fridge, to more of a cutesy home exhibition. Even renters with strict rules not to hang anything on the walls have the means to do this: embrace the Command strips or go full kitsch with a kitchen fridge magnet gallery.

OPPOSITE Etheline Tenenbaum would approve of the unadulterated kitsch in this bright living room. From the warm orange and pink tones to the clashing prints and eclectic decor.

GO TONAL AND GET COLOUR DRENCHING

Consider Etheline's red-and-pink outfits and you'll see that this is a woman who embraces tonal colour schemes extremely well. Presumably, it's she who's supposed to have decorated the family home, because the mansion is a vision in warm colours. The hallways, drawing room and ballroom are all a flush of pencil-rubber pink and faded vermilion, which will look knowingly kitsch recreated in any modern front room. Contrast white mouldings for some zingy respite from pigment and try such tonal combinations as blue and purple, blue and green, or yellow and orange. Try to choose colours that look like an evolution of one another: make one lighter hued and one darker to best salute the Anderson agenda.

Alternatively, you could engage in a spot of colour drenching in which you paint the walls, radiators and ceiling in the same hue. If you're on the big project wagon you could even source furniture and soft furnishings in that colour, too. Something far out of the primary colour box is best for this: pistachio-green, cornflower-blue, rust-red or rich brown will make it look as though you raised genius children.

ABOVE LEFT Colour drenched in Dirty Red and Dirty Peach from YesColours and complemented by a tonal rust sofa, this room is brought together by the subtle placement of a palm in verdant green.

—

ABOVE RIGHT Tonal drenching is achieved in this vibrant living room by matching the sofa to the wall colour. Ornate framed prints and mismatched patterns add that quirky Tenenbaum charm.

GO ANTIQUING

Mid-century modern is king in most of Anderson's films, so get acquainted with your local flea markets, vintage shops and antiques stores. Sure, plenty of brands make imitation designs that hark back to the late 19th and early 20th centuries, but few can deliver the same quality, nor can they be as convincingly worn-in as the chairs and tables in the Tenenbaum mansion.

Look for dark woods like those seen on the chocolate-bar panelling of the Tenenbaum dining room, and seek out sofas and armchairs in variegated antique patterns similar to the golden one Richie and Margot sit on in the reunion with their dad. Smaller pieces can be similarly sourced: a brass floor lamp, a raffia rug, a bold shower curtain. Prioritize interesting colour and texture in fabrics and the bronze quality of oak and brass in accessories.

MORE IS (MOSTLY) MORE

Disciples of Margot Tenenbaum's style know that a lot of effort goes into looking that nonchalant. So it is with interior design; the parrot lamp you picked up for your shelves might look incongruous, but it also appears at home set at a right angle to the vintage tennis racket, which in turn is a tonal complement to the wood of the shelf itself.

By virtue of their eccentricity and generational wealth, the Tenenbaums' house is not quite as uniform as many of Anderson's other sets, but it's still extremely clean and organized in its own way. Lights may be mismatched, but they all work as a lovely symmetrical whole. Add a standing lamp in one corner of the lounge and balance it with a wall-fitted light at the same height a little further along, and yet another in a third corner, if you want to imitate the lamp-heavy Tenenbaum house.

MIX OLD AND NEW

Vintage suits with tennis sweatbands and fur coats with Lacoste T-shirts: the high and the low, traditional and modern go together seamlessly in Anderson's vision of 1970s New York, and not only in wardrobe. Bring this vibe – an essential representation of kitsch – into your living room with similar contrasts. Heavy yellow curtains like those seen in the background of the fourth-floor ballroom would look marvellous framing an alcove containing your high-tech sound systems. How about a nightlight in the shape of a cartoon character nestled among your liqueur bottles on an antique bar cart? This could even work by adding contemporary throw cushions to a vintage sofa.

EMBRACE THE CLASH

Etheline and Royal didn't let Richie paint directly on to his walls just so that you could um and ah about whether to branch out with leopard print and tartan. So-called bad taste is exactly what to go for here: if you love it, add it in. You'd be surprised at how a collection of things that look as though they should never go together in a million years coalesce in the hands of someone who has taken care in choosing them. Some reassurance: in the business of clothes and interiors, stripes and animal print are considered neutral, colour almost always looks better than grey and beige, and as long as you keep the coffee table dusted, it can never hurt to add a bizarre curio beside your hardback books.

ABOVE Interior designer Hollis Loudon brings together an eclectic mix of prints and patterns to create surprising harmony and beauty in this stunning living room.

—

OPPOSITE Vermillion walls, mixed media and clashing prints: the home of Sarisa Munoz (@indigoleopard) is straight out of the Etheline Tenenbaum playbook.

BOHO YOUR SOFA

Not everyone can do up their entire front room, nor is it necessary; instead, you could focus on just your sofa. If you're in the market for a new one, look for chintzy, corduroy or variegated floral patterns in interesting colours, and if you're not, consider draping such patterns across the seats and backs by way of throws. Then get thinking like a Tenenbaum by choosing more throws and shopping for interesting cushions in surprising designs. If your sofa has feet, you could swap them for something with a little more panache: clawed, antique, or even halved tennis balls.

THE ROYAL TENENBAUMS IN OTHER ROOMS

The bathroom

We don't get much of a view into the bathrooms in the Tenenbaum mansion, but the one that Margot and husband Raleigh St Clair (Bill Murray) share is a great source of inspiration for those who prefer their kitsch a little more restrained. Etheline may have chosen an avocado or pale pink tile for her en suite, but the St Clairs opted for plain brick tile that matches the free-standing tub. Instead, colour comes through in the details: a bright floral shower curtain, a stack of colourful towels and, of course, a vintage rotary phone for any impromptu landline chats with the adopted brother you're obsessed with.

OPPOSITE The bathroom shared by Margot Tenenbaum and Raleigh St Clair is positively ascetic compared to the mansion in which we spend most of the film.

—

BELOW A grown-up-sized indoor tent? Richie's makeshift accommodation in the family living room allows Anderson to explore one of his favourite spaces – the den.

The den

Though Richie's makeshift tent is a little sad in the context of his story, it is still a delightful thing to behold, and something that anyone with a spare closet room or office corner they don't mind making more fun could use as inspiration. Create the effect by stringing hangings and throws from the ceiling and pinning them to fall like the ceiling of a tent. Instead of a big light, opt for a couple of antique and/or novelty side lamps, or else go fully childlike with a disco ball or a globe light like Richie's. You should also decorate it with things that bring you joy. For Richie, that's a photo of his family, a record player, his collection of cars and a few of his tennis trophies. For you that could mean a shelf of knick-knacks that remind you of different places you've been and experiences you've had: baubles you've found on holiday, greetings cards that are particularly meaningful, inherited bric-a-brac and so on.

THE ROYAL TENENBAUMS

AFTERNOON TEA

Give your craft-shop member's card a dust and head out for card to ink your 375th St Y invitations on – it's time to imagine the kind of party Margot Tenenbaum might have thrown had she not been plagued by malaise and seemingly without friends. Other than Royal's three daily cheeseburgers with French fries and Richie's flamboyantly garnished and liberally peppered bloody Mary, we don't see a lot of eating and drinking going on in the Tenenbaum household. That means we can speculate in order to invent thematic dishes that might have been present during Margot and her much older but just as sad husband Raleigh St Clair's garden tea together.

In a family this eccentric, it doesn't feel too much of a stretch to add a lot of sour flavours to the mix for a bittersweet profile. Sweetness in biscuits and cakes should only serve to complement their unusual flavour profiles; who can say if the chocolate cake the family shares in the dining room isn't made with sour cream? Some would argue that the traditional elevenses fare is better made that way in any case.

SUGGESTED DISHES

SAVOURY

Gherkin sandwiches (thinly sliced like a cucumber equivalent), cheeseburger sliders and fries with sauerkraut

SWEET

Sour cream chocolate cake, black cherry butter biscuits, Viennese whirls

TABLESCAPE

Place cards are a fun way of introducing crafts into your get-together, and in a *Royal Tenenbaums* theme, that could come in the form of a Sweet Afton's Virginia cigarettes packet filled with rolled-up paper 'cigarettes' with fortunes written on them. In line with the actual dining room in the film, the tablescape should be unfussy but peppered with different shapes and sizes of glassware. If you prefer something effusive then go with a tablescape that mimics the house as a whole: make the tablecloth red, the napkins pink and the afternoon tea stand brass, then add celery in jars in place of flowers.

PLAYLIST

— **Nico**, 'These Days'
— **The Clash**, 'Police and Thieves'
— **Mazzy Star**, 'Happy'
— **Joni Mitchell**, 'California'
— **P J Harvey and Thom Yorke**, 'This Mess We're In'
— **Portishead**, 'Sour Times'
— **The Velvet Underground**, 'I'll Be Your Mirror'
— **Silver Jews**, 'Random Rules'
— **Fugazi**, 'I'm So Tired'
— **Elliott Smith**, 'Needle in the Hay'

BLOODY MARGOT

Richie's bloody Mary appears three times in *The Royal Tenenbaums*, and each time it's accompanied by a personal supply of black pepper. In this version, sub in some of the Tabasco for more pepper and top off with a celery stalk as a garnish.

— 75ml (2½US fl.oz) vodka
— 400ml (13½US fl.oz) tomato juice
— A dash of Worcestershire sauce
— A dash of Tabasco
— A pinch of celery salt
— A squeeze of lemon
— More than the advisable black pepper
— Ice
— Celery stalk

Combine the ingredients, except black pepper and celery stalk, in a tall glass with the ice and stir. Finish off with the black pepper and celery stalk.

DREAM GUEST LIST

— Iris Apfel
— Alexa Chung
— Sigmund Freud
— Anton Chekhov
— JFK
— JD Salinger

HOW TO CREATE THE PERFECT GALLERY WALL

Unless you want to fill every space from skirting to ceiling with frames, don't worry too much about planning out where each individual picture will go. Instead, treat it like an ongoing project, and allow patience and serendipity to fill the gaps for you. Try to resist buying a wholesale gallery wall; if you go for all the flash on the sheet then you will have cheated yourself out of the pleasure of finding new gems and building a collection over time.

1. **Select your wall:** A big swathe of space is great, but since you can frame anything for a gallery wall – cinema and gig tickets, plane stubs, miniature crochets – so is a tiny area above a desk or armchair. Think outside the box, you could spread your gallery feature around the corner of a room, or either side of – and over the top of – a door frame.
2. **Mix your mediums:** Pretty much anything that you can hang or fix to a wall could go in your new exhibition. Paintings, prints and family photos are the most obvious but there are lots of other things that could go into the mix: mirrors and photo-booth strips; wall hangings or tapestries; lino prints or a key holder (instructions on how to make your own on page 202).
3. **Choose your shape:** The most common style of gallery wall is in a collage format, but you can still get that *je ne sais quoi* with more editorial shapes. Consider a full corner of frames with a 'stairway' of hangings cutting the wall off at a zigzag diagonal.
4. **Keep things straight:** The Tenenbaums' house may be eccentric, but it never looked dirty or cluttered. Hang your frames using a spirit level and be sure to keep them dusted.
5. **Planning ahead:** As with anything like this, it's best to keep things as fluid as you can. You can, however, roughly plan out how your wall is going to go. When you've chosen which shape you want your frames to follow, decide where a few of the larger items will go. This will provide a basic structure which you can then plan smaller frames around, filling in spaces as appropriate. A good idea is to lay your items on the floor and take your time to move them into a pattern that works for you. Keep in mind that this is a project that will evolve over time, so don't worry too much! There's no way of envisioning an entire wall unless you already have every single piece of ephemera you want to put up there, and you want to avoid it looking too uniform anyway.

Cottagecore

The Kitchen

Part 2

The aspirational, temporary home in *Fantastic Mr. Fox* is inside a tree, so it makes sense that it is lush with warm natural light and indigenous wood. In Roald Dahl's day, the associated look might have been referred to as rural charm. In modern parlance, we call it cottagecore, and it flourishes in the rooms most closely tied to the outdoors: summer houses, boot rooms and kitchens. Evergreen in every sense of the word, cottagecore is an inviting genre of decoration that can warm up any space, but particularly those that run the risk of looking clinical with too much laminate and fluorescent light. No one can live in a world of wool and clay built by Wes Anderson's team of crafters, but you can at least evoke that gentleness of light, texture and colour in your human abode.

COSY UP WITH COTTAGECORE

You will probably have seen many a country cottage in the style of *Fantastic Mr. Fox* on your travels across Pinterest, Instagram and interior design magazines through the years, and that's because the picturesque postcard of a simple cottage in the English countryside has been desirable since long before John Constable was painting them. Most people have been coveting a human equivalent of the space Mr and Mrs Fox inhabit since the days when the poor were moved into the crowded cities and the rich bought up land in the country. For most, cottagecore today means gleaming copper pans and bunches of herbs hanging from the ceiling, wooden fittings, cutesy curtains, and perhaps even a smattering of chickens in the garden (albeit not for eating).

PREVIOUS PAGES The bucolic setting of *Fantastic Mr. Fox* provides cottagecore inspiration aplenty.

—

BELOW LEFT A gingham curtain keeps things tidily rustic in the kitchen of Bambi Costanzo's (@number131) 105-year-old West Virginian property.

—

BELOW RIGHT Copper and wood tones bring fox-like warmth to a modern farmhouse kitchen.

—

OPPOSITE True to the main character's natural colouring, *Fantastic Mr. Fox* is abundant in rusty reds, oranges and muted yellows, which are also reminiscent of the 1970s.

COLOUR PALETTE FIRE AND FOX

Colour is one of Anderson's most recognizable tools; you could name each of his feature films from a colour swatch alone. In *Fantastic Mr. Fox*, that tonal palette is a vision of oranges, yellows and chocolates. Not only does this capture the essence of an idealized countryside vista in autumn, but it also pays homage to the time in which Roald Dahl's story was published (1970). More explicitly, of course, it builds out from the fur and hair of the film's animal protagonists.

Think of a cottage and you might first conjure pictures pigmented in acres of green. A warmer palette may come to you only secondarily, yet few things feel more cottagecore than the relentless oranges of *Fantastic Mr. Fox*. Orange, yellow and brown evoke an ancient sense of calm, perhaps because they represent the wood and fire of the hearth, a centrepiece that has coloured our view of what makes a kitchen for centuries. Today, these colours still remind us of cosy weather, changing leaves and a story with a cup of cocoa in front of the flames.

The foxes themselves are a lush kaleidoscope of peach and ginger, with the dioramas of gnarled tree woods and fiery paint jobs an extension of that palette. Placed in those environments, the characters become one with their surroundings: all the better for creating a blended cosiness that the foxes clearly belong in. Even Mrs Fox's prescient lightning paintings are suffused with umber and brown.

While the time these animals live in is – like many Anderson flicks – anachronistic, the crew's dedication to the source material further demands a period palette. Think about it: Mrs Fox's apron dress and Mr Fox's corduroy and wool tailoring scream 1970s, and so do the colours of each *mise en scène*.

RIGHT Renae's (@honinghuffacres) 1898 farmhouse makes exquisite use of natural wood.

—

OPPOSITE Liisi Vali's (@liisivali) 23-m² (250-ft²) cottage on the Estonian island of Saaremaa is liberal in its use of butter- and daffodil-yellows to create an uplifting spring hug of a room.

ALL-NATURAL

The rustic look of Mr and Mrs Fox's house takes cues from the tufted hillock on which the tree stands, running inside and spreading along walls, floors and fittings. Sure, unless you take up residence in an actual tree, you won't be getting the 'original dirt floor' and 'good bark' promised by estate agent Stan Weasel (voiced by Anderson, FYI). What you can imitate is that loving invocation of nature.

In the film, that translates into acorn-patterned wallpaper and sunshine-yellow door frames. Mr Fox's office, which is modelled on Dahl's own writing shed (a vision later extrapolated for Ralph Fiennes in *The Wonderful Story of Henry Sugar*), is similarly warm in leaf patterns and butter-yellows. Even the flint mine that the animals shelter in seems incredibly cosy. How? Through that same acorn design (this time on a tablecloth), traditional crockery, candlesticks, a lit hearth and a handmade garland inspired by a cornucopia (turn to pages 64–5 for a tutorial on how to make your own).

The love of nature also translates into a lot of natural woods. Whether on stools, chairs and tables or ladders and cutlery handles, oak, beech and ash find their way from the outside to the inside everywhere in Anderson's vision of this bucolic community.

PERIOD PIECE

Film purists seeking a large-scale imitation of the above-ground burrow will have to make a decidedly more vintage recipe list for their new kitchen, since the actual still of the room shows a gratuitous 1970s vision of carpet tile and Formica. Like the carnival of brown, orange and yellow, this is presumably an explicit reference to the year in which the original story was published. The signs of the decade abound throughout, from the cutesy tablecloths to Ash's love of comic books, to the surfeit of candles (power cuts, anyone?).

ABOVE Rabbit runs the kitchen while Field Mouse hangs garlands in the animals' quaint refugee bunker.

—

OPPOSITE Wicker baskets, check. Crockery on display, check. Candles, check. Mrs Fox would approve of this cosy cottage kitchen.

BRING FANTASTIC MR. FOX HOME

PLANT
Herbs, staghorn ferns and trailing ivy

LIGHT FITTING
Taper candles

COLOUR COMBO
Orange with yellow

SMALL TWEAKS
Curtains at the window and under the sink; a vintage runner rug in a galley kitchen; dried flowers; vintage paintings of a country landscape; raffia or wicker baskets

BIG PROJECTS
Stone or parquet wood flooring and Afghan rugs; plants on every surface; an antique lamp and candles fitted into a chandelier; a countryside mural; wooden beams.

MAKE YOUR FLOORS MORE MEDIEVAL

Take the overall look of the film as opposed to our narrow insight into the real dioramas on display, and there's a world of country cottage referencing you could be doing. With a large budget, it means stone or parquet wood floors covered in antique or Afghan rugs. In this sense, our ancestors who toiled in castle kitchens had the right idea, with their practical decoration morphing into aesthetic preference through the years. Those without impossible bank accounts can still add a rug; even a runner will look well in a galley kitchen.

Cleaning logistics will, however, have to be considered, and those with young children should choose machine-washable rugs, of which there is now an impressive range of designs to choose from. If, for mopping reasons, you'd simply rather have some sort of tile, make it an eye-catching pattern in brown and beige.

OPPOSITE Vintage steel drawers, a retro splashback and a beautiful rug would make this Bluemont Virginian cottage (@amycwhyte) a foxes' sanctuary.

GET PAINTERLY WITH PLANTS

OPPOSITE Alexandra (@colorolii) prioritizes original foundations in the antique kitchen she and her black hen share in a village in Poland.

You don't need a PhD in the rules of whackbat to know that plants and flowers can make a difference to your house, but it bears repeating that adding as much foliage as you can is the smartest (and, if you live in a polluted city, healthiest) way to do this. Trailing plants that hang from the ceiling are delightful, sending the kitchen back to its half-inside half-outside roots. Try staghorn ferns for an unusual shape that looks almost as though it was created out of paper for a stop-motion film directed by an aesthetic-obsessed director.

On the countertops, add sprays of dried flowers – they look fantastically vintage, come in a series of aged colours (including lots of peaches, oranges and browns!), and have the added benefit of lasting much, much longer than a fresh bouquet. For the floor, choose plants that you might associate with an English garden: trailing ivy, herbs such as rosemary and mint, and holly for the festive months.

CANDLES, CANDLES, CANDLES!

Most won't have the ability to add a hearth and fire to their kitchen. For starters, you'd have to have an awfully big space. For another, it would require a visit from a chimney sweep (yes, they still exist). Smaller flames it is, then! A smattering of candles – in jars or, even better, as tapers – will still add that primitive comfort of flickering shadows on the walls, plus they can help to neutralize cooking smells.

Extend this dedication to the cosy to your other lighting. If you have an ordinary light fitting, swap the light bulbs for a warmer model. If you're unfortunate enough to have a fluorescent strip light, add a vintage lamp to a kitchen counter to provide a softer option. Leaving the big light off in favour of these flickering and kindly smaller light sources can make the world of difference to what can easily become a clinical room, transforming it from somewhere you operate on food, to a cottage-like place where a rabbit could believably be chef.

COUNTRY LANDSCAPES

So you can't afford to move out of your flat and up to the country. That didn't stop Mrs Fox from bringing the countryside to them once they had lost their new home. You could take her cue and paint (or commission someone to paint) a mural of the countryside, or for renters, it could mean hanging paintings of such scenes (Command strips make it extra easy and avoid messy holes in the walls). Such paintings can be found in antiques or vintage shops, often already in the wood or gilt frames that they look best in.

OPPOSITE Paintings, florals, ceramics and all-important yellow bring an element of kitsch into Sandra Baker's (@the_idle_hands) cottagecore kitchen.

LET'S GET TEXTURAL

Get those natural textures wherever you can. Those wanting a big project could add imitation thatching to a sloped indoor ceiling or install wooden beams to give the appearance of an older, more traditional scullery. Smaller tweaks could include replacing cabinet knobs with wooden ones and hanging copper pans – which reflect light in the style of an autumnal sunset – from the walls.

If you have space, a wooden shelving unit or Welsh dresser ought to contain plenty of wicker baskets and terracotta plant pots. For those with less room, woven hemp or wicker can be repurposed as fruit baskets and under-sink containers.

SHIRK THE DIGITAL

As with many other Wes Anderson films, the love of the analogue is strong. You won't have failed to spot the organized spray of ephemera on the walls in several scenes in *Fantastic Mr. Fox*, from the clippings and sticky notes on Mr Fox's writing shed to the pin boards in Bean's trailer. For the kitchen, this best lends itself to a fridge and/or cork board of artfully (but not too artfully) arranged children's drawings and kitsch magnets.

If you don't already have an Aga (or the money to burn on one) then shirk digital in other, smaller ways: traditional balancing scales and egg timers beat their digital equivalents on every day of the week. Alternatively, why not put up a good old-fashioned clock or a twee set of curtains at the window? Even if you're looking out over a major city road, they'll make everything feel that little bit more *hygge*.

Good morning!
DON'T FORGET TO FEED YOUR SPIRIT

FANTASTIC MR. FOX IN OTHER ROOMS

The dining room

Want to feel as cosy in the dining room as the beavers, opossums and rabbits felt in theirs? Fill the place up with antiques and don't put any pressure on getting anything to match too closely; a hotchpotch of chairs can look as interesting as a collection of plates and serving dishes that have been thrifted over time. A tablecloth is a must, and if you're a fan of the 1970s overtones of *Fantastic Mr. Fox* then you could even get away with one in wipe-clean oilcloth. Bring the tapers you lit in the kitchen through to the table or sideboards (which, if you have the choice, should be wood) or place them in ornate candelabras. Handmade decorations like the garland on pages 64–5 will get you extra credit, particularly during holidays like Christmas, Hanukkah or Eid.

OPPOSITE The model used by Anderson and his team to create the animals' dining room scene, complete with acorn-printed tablecloth and miniature bottle of Dom Perignon.

—

BELOW Something similar to the rodeo print on Ash's lamp would show up 14 years later on a house jacket worn by Edward Norton in *Asteroid City*.

A kid's bedroom

The Wes Anderson vision of a child's bedroom is definitely a stylized one, but it does at least allow for the joys of childhood in the way a bedroom designed by, say, Tom Ford wouldn't. In Ash's room, natural wood has been painted fire-engine red to represent his tween anger, though lighting – here in the form of a cowboy lamp shade (a precursor to *Asteroid City*, by the looks of it) and a hanging solar system – is still soft. Red and orange might seem harsh choices on paper, but softer shades of the latter create a picture that's more akin to living in a smouldering hearth than a gaudy playground. A high sleeper bed like Ash's is a practical choice that leaves plenty of space underneath as well as bringing an elevated, dream-like element to the actual bed position; it feels just like a fox cub to den down underneath or clamber up the ladder to sleep. For the full Master Fox effect, paint a night sky on to the ceiling or wall near their head.

HOST A Fantastic Mr. Fox DINNER PARTY

Invite friends round with invitations as cut-and-stick ransom notes, get that oilcloth table covering out and light the candles, because *Fantastic Mr. Fox* is the most obvious Wes Anderson film for which you should be throwing a full-blown dinner party. Before Badger's flint mine is washed away by cider, the assorted animals of the valley are settling down for a very rustic country meal cooked by Rabbit. It features chickens, geese and ducks roasted alongside peppers and onions, boiled vegetables, cobs of bread and a smorgasbord of cheese. Walter Boggis eats 12 chickens per day, and while that's certainly a little much for one man, there's no denying that the meals he creates with them do look delicious.

We never get to see what the animals might have eaten for dessert at their celebration, but a blueberry doughnut is a great shout for film purists. Beagles love blueberries, and so do most prospective dinner-party guests – particularly when they're absolutely saturated in sugar. Bunce's goose-liver doughnuts might sound stomach-churning, but a doughnut is at least a foodstuff we can all get behind...

Suggested Dishes

MAIN

Roast chicken with roasted peppers and onions

SIDES

Steamed cauliflower, broccoli and carrots; rustic bread and a selection of cheeses

DESSERT

Blueberry doughnuts

TABLESCAPE

Your tablecloth (oilcloth or laminate encouraged) should be a busy garden print showing foliage of some kind – acorns, leaves or flowers – or else a fussy gingham print. Sprays of dried flowers in small bunches could be placed in mismatched vessels, such as repurposed jars and old candle pots. Mismatching your crockery is preferable, but if you have an organized system already in place then give every guest a different colour or pattern of napkin and introduce editorial clutter through a series of colourful candle tapers instead.

PLAYLIST

— **The Beach Boys**, 'Heroes and Villains'
— **The Rolling Stones**, 'Street Fighting Man'
— **Jefferson Airplane**, 'Somebody to Love'
— **The Sonics**, 'Have Love Will Travel'
— **Buffalo Springfield**, 'For What It's Worth'
— **Creedence Clearwater Revival**, 'Fortunate Son'
— **Fleetwood Mac**, 'Little Lies'
— **Simon & Garfunkel**, 'Mrs Robinson'
— **Gerry Rafferty**, 'Right Down the Line'
— **Harry Nilsson**, 'Everybody's Talking'
— **The Doors**, 'Light My Fire'
— **Cream**, 'Sunshine of Your Life'
— **The Band**, 'The Weight'

OLD-REMARKABLE

Burns in your throat, boils in your stomach, and tastes like pure melted gold: here's a twist on an old-fashioned that pays homage to the cider created by Frank Bean's Red Remarkable apples. You should probably consider serving them in emptied juice boxes for the full experience…

— 50ml (1¾US fl.oz) whiskey
— 50ml (1¾US fl.oz) apple cider
— 1–2 dashes bitters
— Apple slice

Muddle the bitters and cider together then add the whiskey and stir. Garnish with an apple slice.

DREAM GUEST LIST

— Tony Robinson
— Mary Berry
— Nara Smith
— Richard E Grant
— Stephen Fry

HOW TO MAKE A COTTAGECORE GARLAND

Badger's flint mine might be the temporary shelter of the animals of the valley, but it still looks like one of the cosiest spaces ever represented in cinema. Nominate your dining room or kitchen to share in the warmth with a seasonal garland like the ones seen hanging above the table of rustic food.

YOU WILL NEED

Materials

Florist wire
Faux leaves (I used maple)
Artificial grapes
Artificial (or real) pine cones
Selection of dried flowers (orange and yellow)
Battery-powered fairy lights

Tools

Wire cutters

1. Using florist wire, twine together small bunches of leaves, grapes, pine cones and flowers – I made 12 bunches for a finished garland length of 50cm (20in).
2. Cut a piece of wire to the desired length of your garland and layout. Twist the fairy lights around the wire.
3. Starting 10cm (4in) in from one end, lay one of the small bunches of leaves against the fairy-light adorned wire, with the stem end towards the centre of the garland. Holding in place with one hand, use florist wire to secure. Continue along the length of the wire, making sure each bunch overlaps the next slightly to obscure the stem ends. Leave 10cm (4in) bare wire at the end to make a hanging loop (see step 4, below). Halfway along the length of the wire, change the direction you are laying the bunches in.
4. Create a small loop at each end of the garland to hang it in your chosen location.

Rajasthani Deco

The

DARJEELING LIMITED

THE HALLWAYS

Part 3

The Darjeeling Limited is a story about three brothers with little in common but a shared set of parents. Owen Wilson, Adrien Brody and Jason Schwartzman as Francis, Peter and Jack Whitman are the narrative heart of Anderson's fifth feature-length film. Yet, to fans of the Wes look, their reconciliation plays second fiddle to the extraordinary Rajasthani design of the train they reconcile on. A fully functional – and moving – film set, *The Darjeeling Limited* is another Andersonian triumph in handmade crafts, with everything from the outer shell to the plates in the dining car made by local artisans. But don't worry if you're not blessed with the talent of the people who hand-painted each of the 500-plus elephants on the titular train. You still have the opportunity to bring some of that Rajasthani deco to your hallways. Can we agree to that?

प्रवेश
ENTRY
सोने के लिए
35-45
TO SLEEP

ROLL OUT THE RAJASTHANI DECO

Pattern, colour and painterly detail spring from every corner of this touring train, which moved up and down the Indian railways as a kind of living exhibition to the talent of local Rajasthani craftspeople. The result is an interesting dichotomy between the spiritual and fraternal enlightenment of these bereaved and abandoned brothers, and the beautiful, boldly pigmented surrounds of India. It's also a glimpse into how a maximalist, Indian-inspired home could look, particularly when used as an antidote to the typically dark and bland hallways.

PREVIOUS PAGES Waris Ahluwalia as the train's chief steward wears aquamarine and green linen to complement the specially painted carriage.

—

BELOW The Whitman brothers, played by Adrien Brody, Owen Wilson and Jason Schwartzman, on the film's second train, *The Bengal Lancer*.

COLOUR PALETTE
BRILLIANT BRIGHTS

Anyone who lives in a Western country will not fail to be charmed by the bright, saturated colour that abounds in every corner of India. That cultural charm is transplanted onto the train, which is bright with sky-blues and spice-yellows, verdant greens and varnished orange-browns. Later, on a different train (*The Bengal Lancer*), the brothers sit together in a car that does for juicy, tonal oranges what *The Royal Tenenbaums* did for pink and red (see page 21).

Patterns and paintings are just as important in these bright environs and include framed images of maharajas and religious figures, 1970s floral Formica, and pillowcases finished with *The Darjeeling Limited* embroidery.

RIGHT Designed by Marie-Anne Oudejans, the private members' club Polo Palladio in Jaipur features a sunshine-bright colour palette that Anderson would approve of. In this maximalist riot, every detail is carefully considered, including the hand-painted murals on the wood panelling for the walls.

EAST–WEST MASH-UP

True to the post-colonial maximalism that is the lifeblood of local artisans, *The Darjeeling Limited* is a collage of heritage influence and a riot of colour and pattern. Being a Wes Anderson project, it is also a stylistic mash-up, incorporating elements of Art Deco seen in Western luxury trains such as *The Orient Express*. We get a glimpse of these references in the crystal chandeliers and ornate wooden bar of the dining car, and in the fleeting shot of Natalie Portman (as Jack's ex) drinking a bloody Mary in a bed with a florid floral headboard.

Ultimately, though, the colours, patterns and handiwork on display are all 100 per cent Indian. Specifically, they are Rajasthani, the region from which Anderson and set designer Mark Friedberg sourced their many hundreds of craftspeople and artists. The paintings typically found on rickshaws and buildings are transplanted on to the exterior and interior walls of the train, with fundamentally Indian motifs such as elephants, tigers and architectural Bombay Deco fonts in full supply. The seldom seen art pieces on the outside of the train actually depict the sets and events of the film itself and are the largest of the commissioned pieces; the richly saturated feel of the world is completed by the attention to even the smallest details, which include embroidered hand towels, minutely painted dinner plates and patterned polyester curtains.

OPPOSITE The interior of *The Bengal Lancer* is a vision in sunset, turmeric and tiger-oranges.

AESTHETIC RISK

Francis asks his brothers to do several things on their trip, and three of those apply to the creative and aesthetic risks Anderson and his team took during the decoration of the train: seeking the unknown, learning about it, and saying yes to everything. No expense or daring seems to have been spared in the clashing colours, exuberantly painted walls and ceilings, and riot of patterns onboard this touring train. Like *The Grand Budapest Hotel*, it is a five-star establishment catering to the sensibilities of the upper classes, and thus it is one long endorphin rush on wheels.

Of course, all of this daring interior design seems risky only to Westerners; in India, paintbox splashes of colour are as commonplace as a cow wandering down the road. Doubtless, Anderson could rest easy in the hands of the local craftspeople, who made everything from the rattan chairs and the tablecloths block printed by hand to the hand-blown glass tumblers. The bold brilliance of the resulting set is testament to their extraordinary talent and their comfort with hues that some other cultures consider bold.

THEMATIC CLASHES

It isn't only the patterns that clash brilliantly in *The Darjeeling Limited*. The three brothers in their greyscale suiting are also in conflict with their surroundings: a Western anomaly in the middle of this visual feast. Next to the train staff in their vibrant saris and turbans, it couldn't be clearer that the trio are out of their depth, their clothing a representation of their spirituality. They acquire local adornments throughout their journey – Indian pumps, a beaded necklace, bindis – but remain in their plain American accoutrements to the very end, so as to keep them rooted in their place of origin.

We never get to meet – or even glimpse – the Whitman patriarch whose catastrophic funeral is the backdrop to the events of the film, but we do see a fair few of his belongings, and it seems possible that he had a more ingrained appreciation for maximalist design than his sons. The highly symbolic luggage that the sons inherit, for example, is a set of brown leather duffels, suitcases, weekend bags and trunks made by Marc Jacobs for Louis Vuitton and illustrated with flora and fauna drawn by Anderson's brother Eric. Hardly the property of a buttoned-up businessman who'd laminate his itineraries…

BRING THE DARJEELING LIMITED HOME

PLANT
Song of India

LIGHT FITTING
Glass rod wall lights in antique brass

COLOUR COMBO
Blue with yellow

SMALL TWEAKS
A ceramic leopard or tiger; a set of patterned curtains; vibrant bunting

BIG PROJECTS
Add bright colours and detail on the ceiling, skirting boards and radiators; source Indian furniture and rugs; buy Bombay Deco grilles.

RELEASE YOUR WESTERN INHIBITIONS

The most important thing of all is to let go of any preconceived notions of how a home 'should' look. Instead search inside yourself and pull out what you would put in the hallways of your home if you could have absolutely anything at all. Greige new-build fodder this is not. Instead, fans of Rajasthani crafts or Bombay Deco should immerse themselves in an Eastern version of *The Royal Tenenbaums'* bohemian kitsch by selecting a pick 'n' mix of soft furnishings, paints and trinkets that make them happy.

In this world, a curtain is more than just a means to keep out light, a rug is more than a warm addition to a cold wood or tile floor, and a table is more than somewhere to keep your mail; each has the potential to create a beautiful picture of your home and leave your mood soaring. Scour local craft shops, Etsy stores and antiques shops to find unusual patterns and curios. The themes don't need to be explicitly Indian or even Rajasthani if you don't want an exact vibe match of *The Darjeeling Limited*, but you should still pick your poisons with all the interest of Jack Whitman purchasing pepper spray.

OPPOSITE The riotous entranceway of creative director India Holmes's home in Highgate, north London, was in part inspired by the blue of the public buses in Kolkata, India.

RIGHT Wall hangings like this bring textural interest as well as colour and pattern to the party in Sarisa's Indigo Leopard home.

—

OPPOSITE Divine Savages offers a muted take on the flora patterns and natural prints that fill the hallways of *The Darjeeling Limited* with its Bloomin' Marvellous wallpaper.

CHERRY-PICK YOUR FAVOURITE INDIAN PATTERNS

The soft furnishings on the film set of the train were block-printed by hand, but even those who don't have a trip to Jaipur booked can get their hands on patterns like these. The key terms you need to be armed with in your search for appropriate tiling, jute rugs, wallpapers and curtains include: Kalamkari, which usually presents as ornate, hand-painted animals and flora; Bandhani, which makes colourful, repeat print tie-dye textiles; and Ajrak, which involves block printing in patterns Westerners might most closely associate with paisley. For an authentic Indian rug search for words like 'Kashmir' and 'Jaipur'.

For the look of the film without the exacting props, choose bright colours and interesting patterns. Natural inspirations are great, but so are zigzags and depictions of constructed objects, such as houses. Remember, too, that these patterns can exist on smaller as well as larger projects: a wall hanging, say, or a bright ceramic sitting tiger, or simply a small trinket dish to keep keys and loose change in.

OPPOSITE A hotel in the Rajasthani capital of Jaipur, the Villa Palladio is a feast for the eyes, where the Art Deco of *The Grand Budapest Hotel* meets the exquisite crafts of local artisans.

—

RIGHT A witty Hollis Loudon project in the USA extends the bright wallpaper and ceramics from the living room through to the hall, creating a sense of flow through the home.

IT'S ALL IN THE DETAIL

The handiwork of talented painters is all over the fabric of Indian society, and that love of the elaborate continues on the walls of the train, both inside and out, as well as on the ceiling of the dining car with its night sky scene and lush foliage. Nowhere should be safe from you and your paintbrush: ceilings, walls, floors...even skirting boards, radiators, tiles and picture rails could be the canvas for your next brush with nature. Or, for the look of practised detail without the effort, get on your ornate wallpaper game. If you're in a rental, removable wallpaper is a great option, or hang bright depictions of flora and fauna instead. You could also add pattern via curtains. No need for a window to do this; you could hang drapes on either side of a hall table or as a tent-like draping from the ceiling.

MIX YOUR MEDIUMS

Mixed mediums are essential to *The Darjeeling Limited*. That means that textures like ceramics, frosted glass, woods, polyester, silk wallpaper and Formica all mingle in the same way as the many patterns and colours. The hallway is the perfect place to play with different textures: tile or wooden floors softened by plush or woven rugs; glass side tables and metal hooks; or ornate wooden sideboards and ceramic trinkets. This eclectic philosophy can also extend to discipline. Don't worry about sticking to one kind of art style, but have fun with all the different kinds of Indian artisanry that exist, from batik curtains to traditional ceramics to Bombay Deco grilles.

Hallways can become the forgotten dumping room of the home, but with the same level of care and attention as shown in the sets of *The Darjeeling Limited* you can transform these dull places into welcoming passageways filled with character and colour.

THE DARJEELING LIMITED IN OTHER ROOMS

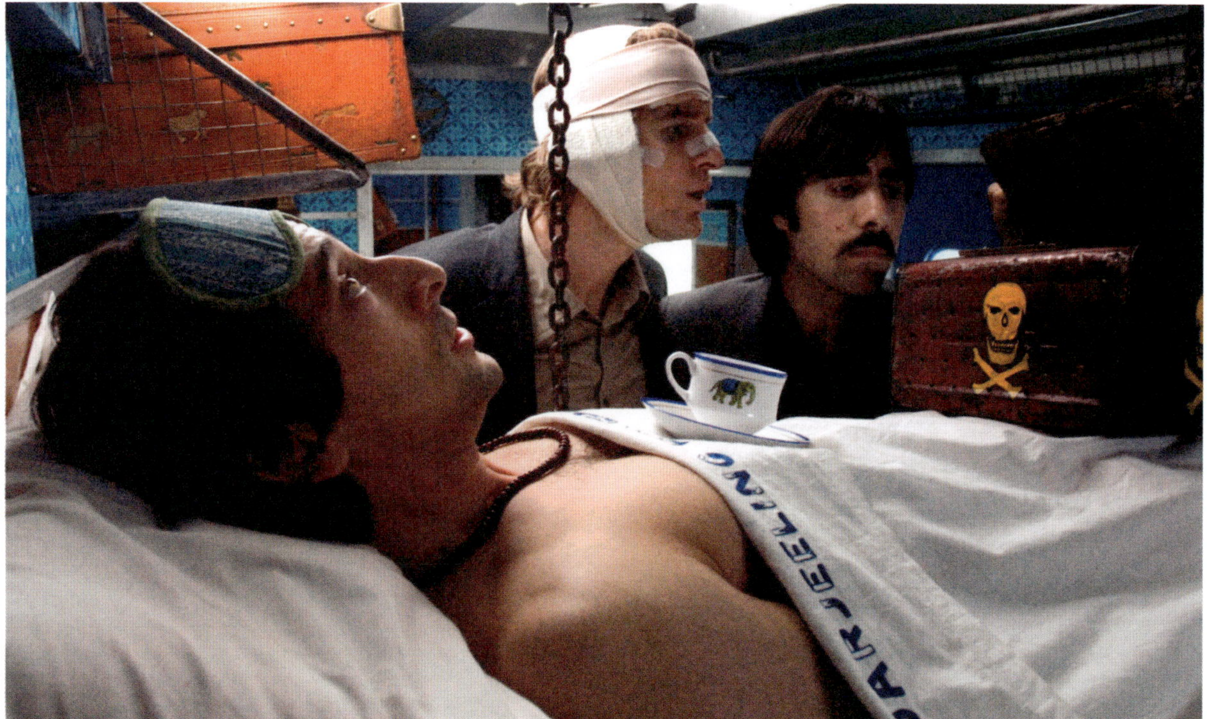

The bedroom

The Whitman compartment consists of rich brown woods and blue block patterns, both of which look lovely in a bedroom space as well as a hall. Some of its cues are mid-century modern, with more tubular lights caged by ornate metal, and floral polyester curtains that are a dream for anyone who enjoys a bit of kitsch. The top bunks are suspended from chains, which would make an interesting textural addition in the form of a hanging chair or hammock, while functional metal hooks offer the basis for displaying some of your more diaphanous Indian finds.

OPPOSITE Everything from the embroidered branding on the sheets to the tiny painted elephants on the tea cup was created by hand.

—

BELOW Anderson directing in the train's dinner car. Note the embroidery on the tablecloth, the detailing on the menus, and the hand-painted crockery.

The dining room

The dining car of *The Darjeeling Limited* is one of the more intricate and beautiful parts of the set. That's partly because of all those hand-painted props, which – visible or not – breathe life into their surroundings. Equally ambitious is its ceiling, which is lusciously painted like the night sky. You can live these dreams in miniature with smaller choices. Whether you have a dining room or a dining area within the kitchen or lounge, you can borrow from the genius of these artisans by introducing patterns and whimsy through something as simple and interchangeable as your place mats. Equally, you can invite a sense of *Orient Express*-like opulence by thrifting for a new set of polished matching cutlery. As for the ceiling, the so-called fifth wall, you could avoid the difficulty of an artisanal-level transformation by paying attention to it with a simple coat of paint, either in the same hue as the walls for a spot of colour drenching, or in something complementary or tonal.

HOST A DARJEELING LIMITED DINNER PARTY

It's a point of contention in the Whitman family that the eldest brother orders food for his siblings, but guests at your *The Darjeeling Limited* dinner party will have no choice but to go with what you've prepared for them. Have your menu printed and laminated for the table, complete with forensic detail on the dishes you'll be serving. Like the choice in the dinner car, chicken, fish or lamb laal maas (a Rajasthani version of rogan josh) will most closely imitate the film, as will soup, which from the looks of the brothers' finished bowls is Indian tomato. Roti is essential, and so is the choice of pudding: cake or cookies.

SUGGESTED DISHES

MAIN
Chicken, fish or lamb laal maas

SIDES
Indian tomato soup, bajra rotis

DESSERT
Cake or cookies

TABLESCAPE

A turmeric-yellow tablecloth with rattan place mats as the foundation, crystal candlesticks and/or antique lamps as lighting, and a couple of framed pictures of maharajas will bring the lustrous Indian feel of *The Darjeeling Limited* dining car. To honour the colours of the film, add sky-blue napkins and perhaps put up floral-printed nylon curtains on the back of each chair – or on the wall beside the table if you want to go all out. Finish with cut-glass tumblers and place cards painted with elephants. For extra points, source yellow plastic bags in which to offer your table favours.

PLAYLIST

- **The Kinks**, 'Strangers'
- **Leonard Cohen**, 'Is This What You Wanted'
- **Claude Debussy**, 'Claire de Lune'
- **The Rolling Stones**, 'Play with Fire'
- **The Kinks**, 'This Time Tomorrow'
- **Jimi Hendrix**, 'Hey Joe'
- **The Kingsmen**, 'Louie Louie'
- **Tommy James & the Shondells**, 'Crimson & Clover'
- **Mitski**, 'Francis Forever'
- **The Smiths**, 'You Just Haven't Earned It Yet Baby'

SWEETEST LIME

What else could you serve to drink but sweet lime? More commonly known as mosambi juice, the tipple that Rita serves to the brothers on the train is a refreshing and non-alcoholic beverage. Let's remedy the latter, shall we?

- 2 sweet limes (or mosambi)
- 2 tsp sugar syrup
- 50ml (1¾ US fl.oz) white liquor of your choice
- Ice
- Sugar and lime to garnish

Squeeze the juice from the limes and muddle with the sugar syrup. Use the empty lime to wet the rim of the glass and roll it in sugar. Fill a cocktail shaker with ice then add the liquor and lime/sugar syrup mix. Shake, pour and garnish with a slice of sweet lime.

DREAM GUEST LIST

- Ravi Shankar
- Satyajit Ray
- Louis Malle
- Amrita Sher-Gil
- Arpita Singh

HOW TO MAKE A SKULL AND CROSSBONES TRINKET BOX

YOU WILL NEED

Materials

Wood (any kind)
5.5mm (¼in) plywood sheet
2 small butt hinges
8 screws
Wood paint (in colour of choice)
Paper (to draw design template)
Chalk paint
Varnish

Tools

Dust mask, ear protectors and eye protection
Track saw
Mitre saw
Router
90-degree clamps
Hand saw
Pencil
Tape
Sheet sander in 60-grit and 120-grit
(240-grit if a smoother finish is desired)
Wood glue
Paint brushes

1. Use a track saw to cut the wood to size. The example here is 22cm (8¾in) long, 16cm (6¼in) wide and 10cm (4in) deep. For this, you will need two side pieces measuring 22 x 10cm (8¾ x 4in) in length, and front and back pieces measuring 16 x 10cm (6¼ x 4in).
2. Use a manual mitre saw to cut 45-degree angles on each joining edge (shortest edge) to form the box corners.
3. Dry fit the pieces to check alignment, then use a router to cut a 6mm-wide (¼in) groove 8mm (⅓in) from the bottom edge of the internal facing sides of all four sides of the box. Cut to a depth of approximately 8mm (⅓in) and secure using 90-degree clamps.
4. Using a hand saw, cut a piece plywood sheet to size for the bottom of the box. To size this, mark a pencil line around the perimeter of the dry-clamped box, then adjust the size to allow the cut piece to slot into the precut grooves snugly.
5. Once cut to size, fit in place and dry-clamp to check for size.
6. Tape the box on each corner, then either measure the final perimeter of the box, or use a pencil to draw around the perimeter on to a piece of the remaining wood. This will give you accurate measurements for the box lid.
7. Using a hand or track saw, cut the box lid to size and sand all aspects using a sheet sander, first with a 60-grit and then with a 120-grit (240-grit may be used for a smoother finish).

8. Untape the side pieces and sand in the same way as the lid.
9. Lay out the sides ready to glue.
10. Following the manufacturer's guidelines, apply wood glue to the 45-degree angles of each side piece and fold together while setting the plywood bottom of the box into place.
11. Secure firmly using tape and 90-degree corner clamps while checking that the box is square.
12. Allow the glue to dry overnight, then remove the clamps and tape. Set the lid in place ready to attach the hinges.
13. Place the hinges approximately 3cm (1¼in) inset from the edge of the lid on each side and secure with screws.
14. Paint the entire box, including the interior, using two coats of wood paint in your preferred colour.
15. Draw a skull and crossbones design in pencil on to a piece of paper (you could also print one), cut out and check for size on the lid. Then place the template on the lid and trace the outline with a pencil, pressing firmly to softly score the wood underneath.
16. Use chalk paint in your colour of choice to fill in the outline.
17. Allow the paint to dry, then apply varnish to seal.

European Charm

THE OFFICE

Part 4

The French Dispatch columnist Herbsaint Sazerac (Owen Wilson) may not provide the most flattering of portraits of the magazine's setting, Ennui-sur-Blasé, but in the hands of Wes Anderson, even the more unsavoury elements of this fictional French town are aesthetic putty. In the film's journey through the final issue of *New Yorker* stand-in *The French Dispatch*, we see this small town, warts and all. And yet, when the surroundings are this sumptuous, and the adoration of a certain European charm is so evident, even a smattering of rats in the street can seem rose-tinted. In this 2021 outing, Wes proves that anything – even an office overflowing with paperwork – can be quaint when viewed through the lens of a detail-obsessed Francophile.

FRENCH DISPATCH
1
2-3
ROEBUCK WRIGHT
4-5
24-25
26-27
34-35
FILLES
GARÇONS

10-11
12-13
14-15
16-17
18-19
20-21
8-9
BERENSEN
CADAZIO
ROSENTHALER
38-39
40-41
42-43
44-45
46-47
62-63
64-65
66-67
68-69
72

BE CHARMED BY EUROPEAN DESIGN

From its prison to its red-light district to its bistros, Ennui is a prototypical French town (indeed, the film was shot in Angoulême in southwestern France). And yet the sets built within it represent a dream of the country that could exist only in the mind of Anderson, who has an apartment in Paris as well (as we already know) as a predilection for beauty. Shot in sections, like the magazine it depicts, *The French Dispatch* is loyal to the French art of flea market antiquing and the charming bric-a-brac so at odds with the minimalist chrome of the USA in the mid-20th century. Watching it will have no doubt convinced you to réarranger your working space to mimic that of Editor-in-Chief Arthur Howitzer Jr (Bill Murray)'s office. Whatever you end up with, make it look as though you made it that way on purpose, won't you?

PREVIOUS PAGES *The French Dispatch* flat plan, with a level of attention to detail and perfection that only Anderson could bring, has echoes of the gallery wall in *The Royal Tenenbaums*.

—

BELOW Bill Murray's Arthur Howitzer Jr matches his shirt to the panelled walls of his editor's office.

—

OPPOSITE A masterclass in colour blocking, Tilda Swinton's shades of orange pay homage to the 1970s.

COLOUR PALETTE
ORANGES AND LEMONS

Like many of Anderson's films, *The French Dispatch* takes place during the latter half of the 20th century, this time in 1975 as the titular magazine takes its last breath. Accordingly, the offices of the publication are run on analogue, populated by teak and mahogany furniture, and very, very yellow. They may be profuse, but, like Anderson's surreal tableau of stories, these fairytale interiors are firmly rooted in reality. Some examples: in the 1970s, writers were more likely to have their luxury writing retreats expensed; the editor, too, was more likely to be in possession of a grand wooden desk. Youth revolts were more likely to come with poetic manifestos; the corridors of a working space had a much higher chance of being slathered in buttercup-yellow paint. Perhaps then, art journalists could bribe their way behind prison walls; filing would certainly have been done using towering cabinets.

Rebellion and revolution aside, aesthetic fans of the period will find inspiration everywhere, particularly in the 1970s colour palette that abounds in the film. They'll find it in the orange gown worn by Tilda Swinton's art critic J K L Berensen, as well as her orange hair and the orangey wood panelling seen behind her during her keynote on Rosenthaler; in the colour-drenched yellow tones of the newspaper offices; and in details as small as the frosted glass panel of the editor's door.

FRENCH 'SPLATTER SCHOOL'

Adherent to Moses Rosenthaler (Benicio Del Toro)'s abstractions or not, you can't help but fall in love with the charming hotchpotch of colours and patterns seen throughout *The French Dispatch*. From scattershot vintage drawers in Sazerac's apartment to the dizzying number of prints on show in Roebuck Wright (Jeffrey Wright)'s colourful flat, there is organized chaos everywhere. That is nowhere more true than in the offices of *The French Dispatch*, where brimming wastepaper baskets, lidded archive boxes, and pin boards flush with notes are as prevalent as chairs and tables. No doubt you were impressed by the way in which Anderson and his team (Adam Stockhausen on production design) created synergy in spaces that are so often head-achingly chaotic in reality.

In part, this splendid cross-section of liberal French living also mirrors *The French Dispatch* itself, which treats its writers with an almost utopic indulgence: everything is in its right place, but creativity and expansiveness are always lavishly rewarded.

OPPOSITE The apartment of Herbsaint Sazerac is a love letter to analogue, what with film cameras, paper maps, stacks of books and a pushbike all among the props in frame.

—

ABOVE 'The best living writer in quality of sentences per minute' composes on a typewriter with his right hand while writing in pencil with his left.

ANALOGUE

Animation, stage props, paintings, radio…to date, *The French Dispatch* is the Wes film with the most examples of analogue and/or traditional techniques. Together, they build a towering stack of tricks that lend an extra layer of period authenticity. One can imagine that Wes is no fan of e-bikes, vapes or chess.com; this is a project that is firm in its love of fixed-speed bicycles, cigarettes and chessboards. Then there are the typewriters, the adding machines, the paintings, the pottery, the film cameras, the Morse code, and so on. Assembling an 80-page magazine with a cork board and a stack of legal pads is not the easiest way to do things in the 21st century. Nor is building each set with painstaking prop research and sleights of hand – but they are both still the most satisfying and beautiful.

BRING THE FRENCH DISPATCH HOME

PLANT
Palms

LIGHT FITTING
Antique wooden table lamp

COLOUR COMBO
Yellow with blue;
yellow with pink

SMALL TWEAKS
Add a spinning globe;
display books and magazines;
paint a feature wall;
hang framed photos and maps

BIG PROJECTS
Invest in antique filing cabinets and other traditional shop fittings;
panel a wall in yellow wood;
install a parquet floor.

LOOK INTO TRADITIONAL SHOP FITTINGS

What Sazerac's house, the Ennui-sur-Blasé police station and the *French Dispatch* offices have in common – besides an obsessive focus on symmetrical framing – is traditional shop fittings in oak and mahogany. You might recognize these exactingly made towers – which range from minutely sectioned chemist drawers to industrial filing cabinets to capacious wooden lockers – from opticians, jewellers and haberdashers that have retained their vintage furniture. Most vendors will have acquired these beautifully built pieces during the Victorian and Edwardian eras but collectors and aesthetes like you can still find authentic antiques or discerning copies in specialist shops.

If you have the money to save up for even one of these design spectacles, few things could lend your working space more gravitas or *French Dispatch* European charm. On the more affordable end of the spectrum, consider buying something small like a vintage in/out tray or a spinning globe, both of which also feature in the Howitzer office.

OPPOSITE Laura Karasinski's office makes a cork board the focal point of a wood and raffia space.

BIS AUF
DIE SYPHILIS.
Champion
BAR CAMPARI
VIENNA
HOTEL ROTHAUS LUCERNE
SUISSE
PLAY

FILING CABINETS WORK, TOO!

It isn't exactly accessible – either on the financial or the space front – for most to go out and buy an authentic double-wide cabinet, but you won't go far wrong with a more modern filing cabinet in steel. It may say more 1970s than 'impressive relic still knocking about in the 1970s', but that isn't a bad thing whichever way you cut it. Look for either beige or bright colours, such as yellow or orange, and always prioritize buying pieces that do something interesting with their handles – because it's unlikely that Arthur Howitzer Jr would ever have been seen dead with something other than glass knobs or cup handles. Remember: even if you can't find the perfect cabinet at the right price, you could always paint one yourself and find some cheap handles to replace the existing ones.

BRING YOUR BOOKS INTO YOUR ORBIT

Books and papers are stacked on every surface in the sets of *The French Dispatch*, and while that may not make you look forward to dusting with much enthusiasm, there's no denying how charming it looks. Move some books from a shelf elsewhere in your home and group them by spine colour; you could, for example, gather all your orange Penguin books together as a backdrop to your desk or on top of a cupboard or cabinet. Collect the magazines you subscribe to in this space, too, perhaps in a wicker basket or a wooden magazine rack. Lastly, coffee-table books aren't just for the living room; stand them up along a skirting board or inside a cabinet for a bibliophile-approved look.

BELOW The placement of some tomes on the floor adds a nonchalant look preferable to buying a new bookcase.

—

OPPOSITE The higgledy-piggledy stacking of the bookshelves in this home office brings warmth and personality to the space, set off by the warm brown tones of the paint that echo the natural woods.

GET INVENTIVE WITH YOUR WALLS

Like *The Royal Tenenbaums* and *Moonrise Kingdom* before it, *The French Dispatch* loves a gallery wall, here arranged around the window behind Howitzer's desk in an arc of framed photographs, postcards and even illustrations that have been drawn directly on to the wood. If nothing else, this shows us that you don't need anything bulky to create your own cluster, which can be as big or as small as you like.

Most memorably, sprays of ephemera are used in this film on the 'Issue-in-Progress' cork board. Acquire your own and pin with to-do lists, photos and clipped articles ASAP. Maps of Kansas and Ennui-sur-Blasé are frequently found on the walls of the characters' rooms, offering you further inspo, and a blackboard would be not only screen accurate but also indebted to the analogue leanings of the film, and to Anderson's vision at large.

BELOW LEFT Berensen, Sazerac, Krementz and Wright would be proud of the traditional filing and books filling the shelves in Laura Karasinski's office.

—

BELOW RIGHT A cork board? Interior designer Emma Jane Palin prefers a cork wall.

LEFT By colour drenching the wall and radiator in sunshine-yellow, @jolliesandfollies achieves a thoroughly 1970s picture.

ONCE AGAIN, EMBRACE COLOUR

A lot of props and arrangement goes into the *mise en scène* of the *French Dispatch* offices, but the thing that jumps out first is that juicy yellow paint. Anderson and his team have shown how lovely the colour can look on wood panels in a bright, airy space, particularly around windows. Alternatively, introduce yellow (or, for a similar period look, orange or chocolate-brown) via a painted feature wall with a bright floor lamp against it. The blasts of yellow are pulled together by the vintage woods on furniture and floor (note how various shades of wood can work together) and are souped up by bolts of turquoise in glass panelling and rugs. Take these as literal cues if you wish, or try one of the following: deep brown with light blue, grass-green with tangerine, or burnt orange with cream.

THE FRENCH DISPATCH IN OTHER ROOMS

The dining room

Another bright spot in *The French Dispatch*, both literally and figuratively, is Le Sans Blague café, at which student activist Zeffirelli (Timothée Chalamet) and his classmates socialize and put the world to rights. Like the film itself, this space is glaringly yellow, though this time the shade is offset with jolts of red and iron trimmings. This exact effect would be extremely bold in one's dining room, but for those who love the hyperbole of some mid-century designs, it is certainly encouraged. An alternative way to invite the colour combination in is by dressing a dining table with a red tablecloth (make it gingham for a softer effect) and painting a feature wall yellow. Avoid paintbox versions of both colours to swerve the look of a certain fast-food chain, and instead opt for one bright and one pale (for example, primary red with buttermilk yellow). Finish by adding a yellow metal cabinet to store crockery.

OPPOSITE Le Sans Blague (translating to 'The No Joke') is the kind of European bistro that *The French Dispatch*'s entire production design revolves around.

—

BELOW Writer Roebuck Wright's apartment has visual echoes of the lobby of *The Grand Budapest Hotel*.

The living room

One of the most beloved stills of *The French Dispatch* depicts Jeffrey Wright's character perched on his floral couch while Bill Murray-as-Howitzer suggests edits to his article. It endures because the shot takes in a riot of colour and pattern that somehow still manages to appear urbane and classic. In this way, as well as in its use of ornate rugs and pink with red and yellow, it seems to reference *The Grand Budapest Hotel*. It is unlikely that Wright has a television in this room, but if you do, simply bookend it with points of interest that reference this cerebral space: a palm in an interesting pot on one side and an ornament on a small table at the other. Another instant lift comes in respect of the curtains; adding a polished metal-toned curtain rail and a set of dramatic drapes to your window will give the space an instant shot of elegance.

HOST A

FRENCH DISPATCH

DINNER PARTY

Let's assume you don't live at the top of four winding sets of stairs and a ladder. Then you will have a much easier job delivering your guests their food and drink than the gentleman from the Bar Tabac Journeaux at the beginning of *The French Dispatch*. It wouldn't be a whole lot of fun without some challenges, though, would it? Carry everyone's drinks – whether they be white wine, Coca-Cola, Alka-Seltzer, white wine or...a weird Tabasco oyster shot? – on a round tray from the kitchen and have a truly riotous time trying to recreate the exact meals from the film, or else tap into your inner Lieutenant Nescaffier and invent your own gourmet masterpieces. Roebuck Wright's piece on the commissioner's son was initially supposed to be about a fictional school of food called 'Gastronomie Géndarmique'. Think: is your creation highly portable, rich in protein and able to be eaten with the non-dominant hand only? If not, you may want to reconsider it, because anything else is not conducive to being eaten at a crime scene with paperwork or firearms in the other hand. And please: this is quiet food, so nothing crunchy.

SUGGESTED DISHES

MAIN
Scotch eggs with plum chutney

SIDES
Minced lamb bon-bons (in pastry wrappers), chicken hash

DESSERT
Crème brûlée

TABLESCAPE

The invitation should be a *carte de dégustation* with the dishes printed on one side and a floor plan of your home on the other, and should appear on the topmost plate (of an ornate stack) at each place setting. White candle tapers burned low ahead of time, cut-glass and crystal glassware, and white table linens nod to the luxurious heights that 'Police Cooking' rose to.

PLAYLIST

— **Grace Jones**, 'I've Seen That Face Before'
— **Nancy Sinatra and Lee Hazlewood,** 'Summer Wine'
— **Leonard Cohen**, 'Dance Me to the End of Love'
— **Nouvelle Vague**, 'In a Manner of Speaking'
— **Kate Bush**, 'Oh to Be in Love'
— **Koop and Ane Brun**, 'Koop Island Blues'
— **Serge Gainsbourg**, 'Black Trombone'

TABAC SOUR

A milky, purplish aperitif with a medicinal flavour profile? Sounds like a violet gin sour.

— 50ml (1¾US fl.oz) purple gin
— 25ml (¾US fl.oz) lemon juice
— 25ml (¾US fl.oz) sugar syrup
— 25ml (¾US fl.oz) egg white
— Ice

Shake the ingredients together. Strain and pour.

DREAM GUEST LIST

— Harold Ross
— Jean-Luc Godard
— James Baldwin
— Mavis Gallant
— Rosamond Bernier

HOW TO MAKE AN ENNUI CROCHET COASTER

YOU WILL NEED

Materials

25g (1oz) ball of double-knit wool in colour of your choice (to make a crochet square of 10cm² (4in²))
A contrasting colour of double-knit wool for the text

Tools

Tapestry needle
Crochet hook 4mm (UK 8/US G-6)

Abbreviations used:
ch: chain
dc: double crochet

1. Foundation row: 16 ch.
2. Row 1: 1 ch, 1 dc in each ch.
3. Row 2 (R2): 1 ch, 1 dc in each dc of previous row.
4. Continue with R2 until the square measures approx. 10cm².
5. Repeat to make a second square.
6. For the text, take the contrasting wool colour and embroider '*ennui*' on one of the square pieces with the tapestry needle using backstitch. Leave the other blank.
7. Stack the two squares and sew together around the edges, using either the tapestry needle and an overstitch or a dc with the crochet hook. Secure the thread with a double knot and tuck any loose strands into the crochet square for a neat finish.

Ennui

Whimsy

MOONRISE KINGDOM

The Nooks and Crannies

Part 5

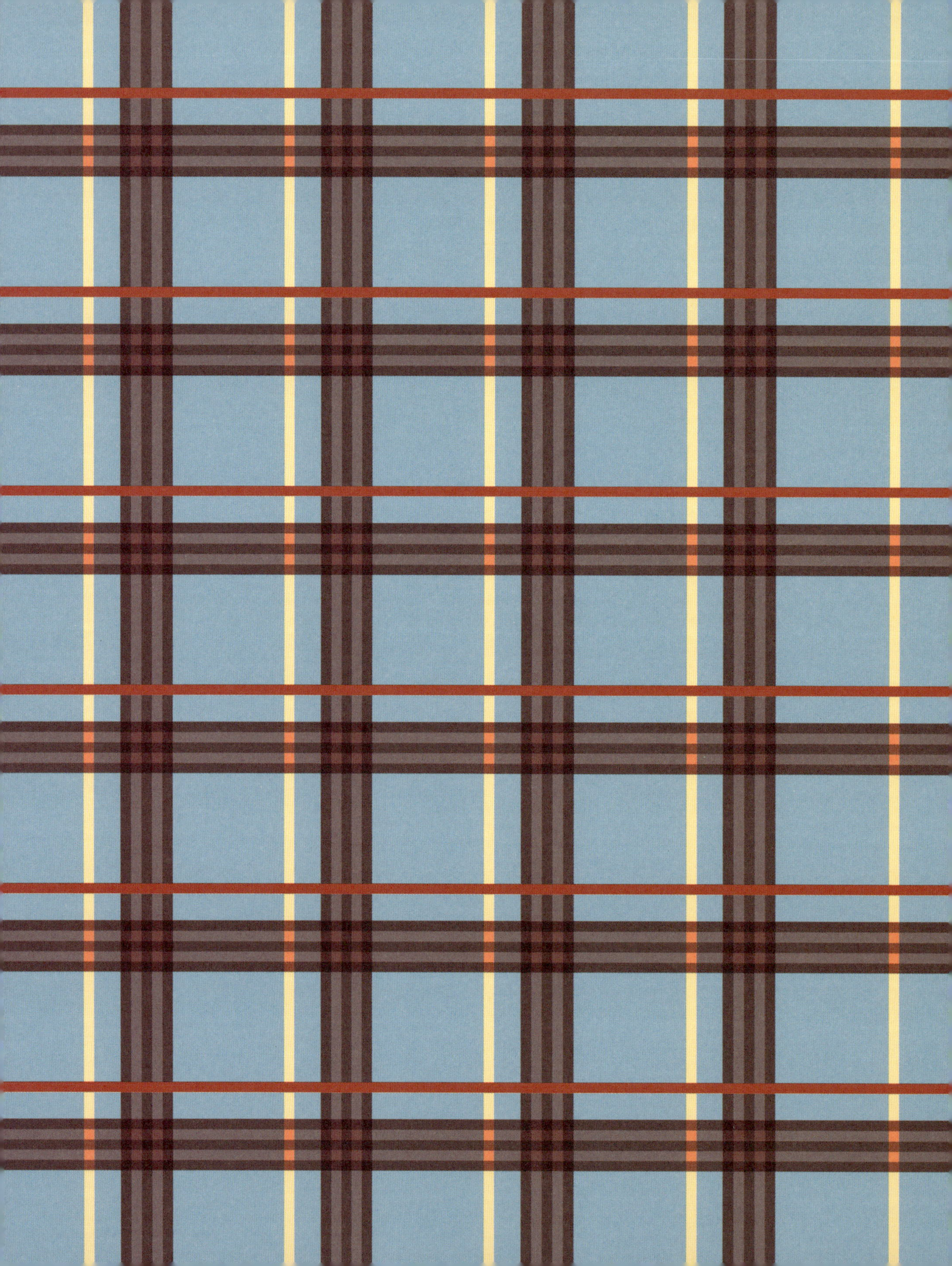

Anyone who visited New England as a child, as Wes Anderson did, probably shares his starry-eyed vision of the extreme eastern coastal islands of the United States: a place like the Penzance Isle of *Moonrise Kingdom* where the houses are panelled in cherry-red wood and front porches are shaded by candy-striped awnings. Just 25km (16m) long and without paved roads, this twee little enclave is further idealized by its setting in 1965. The effect is that of a fabled mid-century community rooted in all-American pastimes, a place in which every corner, nook and cranny contains beauty.

WHIMSICAL WONDERS

If the campsites and tents of the Khaki Scouts are magical hideaways, then the seaside dwellings of the story's adults are like fairytale castles. Anderson gives us a thorough look around Suzy's family home, and we see a fair amount of Sam's two foster homes as well – the Billingsley Foster Family for Boys and Captain Sharp (Bruce Willis)'s caravan. In all these spaces, both inside and out, we're given a healthy dose of imaginative interior design that flourishes in the whimsical details. In practical terms, such fancies lend themselves well to doing up the often overlooked corners of your home.

PREVIOUS PAGES You can visit the beach where Sam and Suzy escape to in Fort Wetherill State Park, Rhode Island.

—

BELOW Suzy Bishop is one of many Wes Anderson characters, including Owen Wilson's Dignan in *Bottle Rocket*, with a predilection for using binoculars.

COLOUR PALETTE
SORBET SHADES

Extrapolated from Anderson's own memories of childhood holidays in New England, the Bishops' home is a masterpiece in detail, boasting soft furnishings, records, paint and accessories collected from antiques stores around Rhode Island. We get a satisfying look around it in the opening credits, taking in huge oak bay windows, indoor shingles, ornate blue painted wallpaper, a ping-pong table and a record cupboard-cum-window seat.

Many of these props are plucked directly from the mid-century modern oeuvre, including a gigantic jute rug (very similar to the one in Sam's tent), a red piano, a chequerboard floor and a pastel pantry. Some details are taken from real childhoods. Anderson told *Vanity Fair* that he once found a book similar to *Coping with the Very Troubled Child* in his own father's possession, and that co-writer Roman Coppola's mother used a bullhorn in the house. The rest is Anderson's inner child speaking; if he could envision an ideal holiday at the 'Summer's End' of his childhood, it would look a little like *Moonrise Kingdom*.

The colour palette is correspondingly nostalgic, with retro pastel shades reminiscent of seaside holidays: buttercup-yellow, duck-egg-blue, soft greens and dusky pinks with occasional pops of red.

RIGHT The childlike magic of *Moonrise Kingdom* is expressed in the seaside sorbet shades used throughout the film.

FAIRYTALE NEW ENGLAND

Whether in a massive historical storm or beatific sunshine, Anderson's Penzance Isle setting is cut off from the mainland and accessible only by seaplane or twice-daily ferries. While *Moonrise Kingdom*'s general look is that of 1960s New England, then, it is believable that a little of Anderson's magic could exist in this smattering of faraway isles. As always, everything you can see in this film either actually exists or was constructed by hand specifically for the production, including the three-storey treehouse in Camp Ivanhoe, which necessitated two trunks, including one buried deep into the ground, to be built.

Perhaps here on the fictional Penzance Isle of Anderson's imagination, children can really build treehouses like this all by themselves, tents come complete with jute rugs, you can construct trebuchets in your acres-wide campsite, and you can be married to your sweetheart by a Scout master.

Though there are people who do live in places like the Bishop household, few things could feel as whimsically unreal as living in a lighthouse, so that's where Suzy's family home is set. Its exterior is that of Conanicut Light on Conanicut Island off the coast of Rhode Island, while its interior is heavily inspired by Clingstone House in Narragansett Bay. All told, it is a child's dream brought to life by adults who have the resources to do so.

OPPOSITE Here, *Moonrise Kingdom* references *The Shawshank Redemption* (1994) when Sam is shown to have cut a hole in his tent behind a paper map.

—

ABOVE In one of the fantastical touches that abound in the charming world of *Moonrise Kingdom*, Sam and Suzy calmly survey a 1964 Yamaha YG1 motorcycle, complete with hot-rod flames, suspended from a tree in the woods.

THE IMAGINED

Not everything is sensible period sourcing. Some of the world of Sam and Suzy is pure whimsy, such as the stairs that double as a chest of drawers in the Bishop house, the chimney in Captain Sharp's caravan and the stacks of kitten food Suzy is supposed to have packed into her small vintage suitcase. There's also the miles-long expanse of Fort Lebanon, the firework explosion only narrowly survived by Khaki Scout patriarch Commander Pierce (Harvey Keitel) and Sam's brush with lightning.

Some smaller things are total fabrication, such as the yellow-and-red bus stop painted especially for the film, the handmade fantasy books that Suzy reads from, and the impossibly high budget of the prescient *Noye's Fludde* school play. Classic to Anderson, even tiny details are convincingly invented: the paragraphs that Suzy reads from in her fantasy books, the *Indian Corn* magazine read by Scout Master Ward (Edward Norton) and the titles given to the Khaki Scouts (which include Reptile Patrol and Judo Expert).

WHERE FANTASY AND REALITY MEET

Elsewhere, childhood dreams meet adult's resources, meaning that, as with the three-storey-high treehouse, fantasy can become reality. It starts as small as giving the young boys of the Bishop family a series of ping-pong paddles to choose from, and positioning a bright crocheted picture of the lighthouse they live in on the wall. It includes bringing salt and pepper shakers (but no change of clothes) with you on your camping trip, and having your own letterhead paper at the age of 12.

Unlike surviving in the wild with no coat and living through a lightning strike to the body, these are all things that are physically possible, even if they are highly improbable. It is in this place that we must look if we are to bring the pervasive sense of surreal whimsy in *Moonrise Kingdom* to the real-life corners of your home.

BELOW Suzy's brothers Rudy, Murray and Lionel play Ludo while their father, portrayed by Bill Murray, fetches a hatchet to chop down a tree.

—

OPPOSITE Sam prepares to channel lightning in one of the most fantastical, childlike moments in the film.

BRING MOONRISE KINGDOM HOME

PLANT
Money or umbrella trees

LIGHT FITTING
A miniature antique bronze lamp

COLOUR COMBO
Blue with orange; brown with yellow

SMALL TWEAKS
Add chintz curtains to a corner or around a bed; introduce stripes; get (or buy) into crochet; shop your home and make a shrine of your favourite things

BIG PROJECTS
Build a window seat; make your bed a four-poster; decorate with primary colours.

BUILD A WINDOW SEAT

Anyone who has seen *Moonrise Kingdom* will have dreamed of their own window seat. Suzy can be seen reading in the window of the children's playroom, which makes good use of the low ceiling with a wooden structure containing the family's records and a traditional cushioned platform to recline on. To build something comparable would necessitate a space by a similar window, usually found in a stairway or attic room, but if you don't have a suitably situated window, there are still options.

You could of course build your wooden structure higher with steps built in (extra points if said stairs double as drawers or cabinets), but an armchair or chaise longue below a window will achieve a similar effect. Amplify the look with a bright or chintzy pair of curtains to draw around your nook, an ornate lamp for when the sun goes down, and a shelf full of your favourite books.

OPPOSITE A window seat by a sash window, as seen here, is ideal because it will let in light and, in spring and summer, air.

MAKE DENS OF YOUR CORNERS AND BED

From Richie's tent in the ballroom in *The Royal Tenenbaums* to the prison laundry room-as-bedroom in *The French Dispatch*, Wes Anderson is a big fan of dens and that's no different in *Moonrise Kingdom*, where the ultimate den is explored in the form of the campsite and its tents. If you once made tents out of clothes horses and bed sheets then it's time to apply your adult brain to a more permanent solution: hang patterned throws or curtains from the walls that meet in a corner, or hook a 'princess' canopy from the ceiling and plant an armchair or beanbag inside.

This approach works well around a bed, too, whether it be as four-poster-style hangings or a wooden construction in which the bed nestles. All these projects necessitate ample light, and candelabra-style fittings jutting through the hangings or a chandelier poking through the top are the most Wes. A soft glow can also be achieved through the (supervised) use of fairy lights, which should be pinned around the walls for the most magical, and the safest, effect.

ABOVE LEFT Liisi's (@liisivali) tiny Estonian 23-m^2 (250-ft^2) cottage makes great use of space with a floral canopy framing a miniature gallery wall.

—

ABOVE RIGHT An ordinary bed is made extraordinary by Sandra (@the_idle_hands) with surrounding curtains that match its frame.

CHOOSE PATTERN

As residents of a mid-century modern world imagined by Wes Anderson, none of the characters in *Moonrise Kingdom* is afraid of a little pattern. From the fully plaid interior of Scout Master Ward's tent to the bright yellow stripes in Sam's foster father's kitchen and the painted blue trees throughout the Bishop home, patterns are never shy. Be literal by putting down a tartan stair runner and adding a feature wall with floral wallpaper, or use your best newly uninhibited judgement to add some bright, exciting soft furnishings or rugs. Some smaller ways in which pattern is used successfully in the sets of *Moonrise Kingdom* include the giant colourful jute rug in front of the window seat and childlike novelty curtains by the window. Soft furnishings, such as cushions, throws, rugs and curtains, also offer simpler and more affordable ways to inject a bit of pattern into your home without committing to a full-scale wallpaper. How about choosing a candy-striped sofa to reference the awnings of the Bishop home, and contrasting it with a different colour stripe or different pattern cushion?

LEFT Amanda Cotton's (@Houselust) 1930s home in Watford, UK, is joyful in its use of shape, pastel colours and a vintage fireplace.

TRUST IN HANDMADE...

...Even if you don't trust in your own, that's what commissioning craftspeople is for! Handmade is essential to all Wes Anderson's films, but especially *Moonrise Kingdom*, which takes the self-sufficiency of the Khaki Scouts seriously by making everything from a contraption for flushing the latrine to the bug earrings worn by Suzy. The homely and handmade abound throughout the film, and so they should in your home. Take some cues: the first shot we see of *Moonrise Kingdom* is a pair of scissors hanging on a nail beside a bright crochet of the Summer's End lighthouse. Both of these things could figure in your house, literally if you want, or they could act as inspiration for hanging your own unexpected household items and sourcing your own crochets.

The Bishop home is also notable for the blueish vines and trees that have apparently been painted on to the walls and ceilings. Like the train corridors of *The Darjeeling Limited*, it's lovely if you can do it, but otherwise hang intricate wallpaper featuring flora or fauna, or rely on paintings to hang or prop in the corners of rooms.

OPPOSITE TOP LEFT
Sandra's (@the_idle_hands) sitting room uses a carefully curated selection of antique and artisan touches to bring a quirky character to this elegant living room.

—

OPPOSITE TOP RIGHT
Natasha James's Yorkshire kitchen complete with plush fire fenders adds an extra element of *hygge* with a cosy sofa in a nook.

—

OPPOSITE BOTTOM
Emma Jane Palin creates the dream wardrobe with this incredible use of space, not to mention the gorgeous colour and pattern combo.

DON'T JUST SHOP ANTIQUE, BREATHE ANTIQUE

Moonrise Kingdom looks vintage to us because it sources furniture and props from the era in which it is set. It also relies on the even older surroundings of these homes, and the furniture and props that will have travelled with the families through generations. What this teaches us is that while a beautiful rocking chair can be added to a corner post-haste, it's impossible to create a Suzy Bishop-like home in just one trip to the antiques shop.

Instead, make flea markets, charity and antique shopping a habit that you can satisfy on payday, or at sensible intervals. At these trips you should focus on finding twin light fittings or candle holders, interesting paintings already in their frames (seaside and nautical pictures if you're lucky), ornaments that you love, and, in flusher times, dark wooden and/or rattan furniture that generations can write to their sweetheart from.

SHOP WHAT YOU ALREADY HAVE

You don't need to be buying things to dress up your home à la *Moonrise Kingdom*. For the look of the Shakusky kitchen, dye old net curtains and hang them in a small corner window, or for the lived-in charm of the Bishop hallways, stack some of your books on the floor. Choose a corner that you'd like to soup up, move a frame from elsewhere in the house to the wall there, then add some of your favourite trinkets to a table. This will act as a little shrine to whimsy that should bring you joy every time you look at it.

MOONRISE KINGDOM IN OTHER ROOMS

The kitchen

Adding whimsy to the kitchen is something that most will not have considered. Traditionally, this is a room that is either ruthlessly efficient or a cottagecore wonderland (see pages 42–65). You don't have to change out your whole kitchen to add a little wonder to the traditional heart of the home; just add colour by way of novelty cupboard handles, a bold rug and an even bolder pair of curtains. If you have space, you could introduce a smattering of the ornaments you've collected from charity shops in a designated corner of the countertop or on an open shelf; otherwise use ceiling and wall space for such unexpected additions as framed pictures (or more crochet!) or baskets hung from the ceiling.

The bedroom

If you envisioned an entire space inspired by *Moonrise Kingdom*, as opposed to just one corner, then a bedroom is an ideal candidate. To take the top-floor playroom of the Bishop children as our source material, you'll see how homely it appears – and that's not only because of the low ceiling and sloped roof. The soft lighting is achieved by eschewing the harsh brightness of an overhead light and instead relying on twin, warm-bulbed lights set symmetrically: an easy effect to imitate should you have twin bedside tables. Alternatively, pair lamps on either side of your chest of drawers. The effect of a room in which to hide away from the world is compounded by the appearance of stored books, records and games. Hark back to the clandestine cosiness of your childhood bedroom by bringing some of your favourites in these categories through from the living room (where most people typically keep them).

OPPOSITE Soft yellows, a table lamp and curtains lend this bedroom a warm light. The botanical artwork on the walls is echoed in the soft furnishings.

HOST A *Moonrise Kingdom* PICNIC

If you were going to run away at the age of 12, what would you have packed in your bindle? While you should have some sensible options at your *Moonrise Kingdom* picnic (adults have the unfortunate burden of knowing about the importance of protein), you should also let your child's imagination do the talking. For every sausage roll you serve, there should be a strange yet surprisingly delicious combination of crisps; for every sandwich on its platter, twice as many cakes.

SAVOURY

Whole grilled fish (catching it yourself optional), cheese sandwiches, various flavours of crisp with dips, sausage rolls

SWEET

Every sweet in the supermarket, chocolates, cakes and anything else you loved as a tween

TABLESCAPE

You could serve your picnic at the table, but in deference to the Khaki Scouts you should take this event outside on the grass. Source a striped wool blanket to set your things out on, pack them in a wicker hamper, then serve everything on wooden stumps. You could even tie up sweets and chocolates in handkerchief bindles. Set up a Bluetooth speaker in lieu of a portable record player and get everyone to bring their favourite fantasy/adventure book – if only for decoration. If you have a kitten that you can bring then you'll have out-Wes'ed yourself ...just make sure it doesn't get at the chocolate.

PLAYLIST

— **Elvis**, 'Love Me'
— **Françoise Hardy**, 'Le Temps de l'amour'
— **Plastic Bertrand**, 'Ça plane pour moi'
— **The Undertones**, 'Teenage Kicks'
— **The Beach Boys**, 'Wouldn't It Be Nice'
— **Gillian Hills**, 'Zou Bisou Bisou'

SNAKEBITE KIT

Supposedly, you can quench your thirst by sucking on a pebble, but who would do such a thing when alcohol is available? Only beer, coffee and water are consumed in the course of *Moonrise Kingdom* so, to focus on the first, make your pint a rustic snakebite.

— One part lager
— One part cider

Combine and serve.

DREAM GUEST LIST

— Bear Grylls
— Hal Ashby
— Sir Edmund Hillary
— Lord Robert Baden-Powell

HOW TO MAKE A COUNTERTOP MAILBOX

YOU WILL NEED

Materials

Wood (any kind)
415 x 240mm (16⅓ x 9½in) piece of moderately stiff cardboard (needs to be sufficiently flexible to form an arch without cracking)
Nails
24 tacks
10 wood screws
2 butt hinges
Aluminium sheet
Wood glue
Panel pins
Plywood
Wood paint (in colour of choice)
Wood varnish
Contact adhesive
Felt
Hasp lock with wood screws
Short nut and bolt

Tools

Dust mask, ear protectors and eye protection
Tape measure
Clamps
Hand saw
Plate sander (60-grit and 120-grit sandpaper)
Scissors
Hammer
Jigsaw
Screwdriver
Tin snips
Drill with 25mm (1in) drill bit
5cm (2in) paintbrush

1. Taking the wood, measure a rectangle for the base of your box; the example here is 240 x 150mm (9½ x 6in). Clamp in place and cut to size using a hand saw. Sand the cut piece using first 60-grit sandpaper and then 120-grit sandpaper for a smooth finish.
2. Cut a piece of cardboard to 415 x 240mm (16⅓ x 9½in) using scissors.
3. Using a hammer and nails, tack the cardboard to the bottom of the base wood on either side, creating an arched effect.
4. Trace around one end of the arched cardboard on to another piece of wood, not including the base piece – this will be the back of the box, which will slot in to sit on top of the base piece.
5. Clamp the wood and cut to size using a jigsaw. Attach to the back of the mailbox using two wood screws inserted from the underside of the base piece.
6. To make the door, take a piece of wood and trace around the cardboard at the front end, this time including the base. Clamp and cut to size using a jigsaw. Attach the cut piece using eight screws on two butt hinges at the base of the door/box (so that it opens downwards).
7. Take a sheet of 0.5mm (¼in) thick aluminium and use tin snips to cut a piece to the same size as the cardboard arch (415 x 240mm/16⅓ x 9½in). Set aside.
8. To use the mailbox on the countertop rather than attached to a post outside, it is necessary to raise the base on a plinth. This facilitates the easy opening of the door. To make the plinth, cut two further base pieces but reduce the length by 10mm (⅓in) from that of the original. This allows for a slight overhang at the front to position the hinges.
9. Follow the manufacturer's instructions to glue and clamp the two plinth pieces together with wood glue. Leave to dry overnight.
10. Cut two pieces of aluminium to the same length as the plinth and 20mm (¾in) wider than the depth: 270 x 400mm (10½ x 15¾in). These will wrap around the base. Tack the aluminium to each long side of the plinth using panel pins.

11. Cut two more aluminium pieces to the size of the door and back of the box. Tack both in place to cover the wood.
12. Taking the sheet of aluminium that you cut to the size of the arch, bend the sheet over the cardboard and slide the lower end inside the plinth aluminium overlap. Before securing the aluminium cover to the cardboard, cut away the front half of the cardboard arch to leave a cleaner aluminium finish.
13. Then tack in place, securing the mailbox to the plinth.
14. Next, cut the plywood for the flag: 250mm (10in) long x 50mm (2in) wide tapering to 20mm (¾in) wide, end to end.
15. Slightly round the narrower end (which will be the top of the flag) using 120-grit sandpaper.
16. Mark a point 25mm (1in) from the middle of the bottom of the flag and drill a hole just large enough to allow a short bolt to fit through.
17. Drill a hole in the aluminium body of the mailbox approximately halfway up and 35mm (1⅓in) back from the front edge.
18. Paint the flag using appropriate wood paint, then varnish.
19. Cover the sides and top of the door with a strip of aluminium, tacked in place. Cut a felt piece to size for the interior of the door and secure using contact adhesive.
20. Next, secure a hasp lock to the top front edge of the arched aluminium roof. Pre-drill two holes of 4mm (¼in) to allow wood screws to pass through.
21. Cut a piece of wooden batten 30mm (1¼in) long. This will be used on the underside of the roof to screw the lock into. Screw the hasp in place from above by fixing two screws through the holes in the hasp to hold the batten in place.
22. Pre-drill holes in the front face of the door to allow for the fixing of the second part of the lock with wood screws through the aluminium facing and into the wood.
23. Attach the painted flag using the short bolt and the hole you drilled in step 17.
24. As a finishing touch, add a piece of felt to the front face of the batten using contact adhesive.

Note: This example uses aluminium facing for a traditional US mailbox style, but if you prefer a more colourful Wes-esque vibe, simply paint the cardboard in a colour of your choice.

OPPOSITE TOP What some may call 'awkward shapes', Anderson actively seeks out for his sets. Embrace the quirks in your home and accentuate sloped ceilings with bold prints and colours.

—

OPPOSITE BOTTOM LEFT Pay attention to the in-between spaces in your home – porches, entryways, alcoves. Mixing practical with pretty will make the most of these areas.

—

OPPOSITE BOTTOM RIGHT Colourful touches make even the smallest of corners characterful.

1950s Americana

ASTEROID CITY

THE DINING ROOM

Part 6

A real-estate vending machine, a science fair of the interplanetary variety and an atom bomb that mustn't be detonated without Presidential approval: Wes Anderson wants you to know that *Asteroid City* is a film set in mid-century USA. He clobbers the viewer over the head with this fact not only through explicit content references, which cover the gamut of themes from space exploration to nuclear tensions and loitering spies, but also in the hyper-Americanized stage sets of the play within the TV show within the film.

CASINO

GO GA-GA FOR AMERICANA

One of Anderson's most self-referential and tightly symbolic movies, Asteroid *City* has a lot to say about the melancholy inherent in the American dream. Not everything is as serious as this, though. As ever, this is also a stylized romp that is fastidious in its *mise en scène*, blocking and set design. In its look, it is brighter than *The Grand Budapest Hotel*, more technical than *The Darjeeling Limited* and more stylized than *The French Dispatch*. As a design piece, it is all-American, which most of us can imagine in the context of a diner like The Luncheonette. Gas up the Cadillac, then, for a deep dive into the chrome-soaked world of 1950s Americana and how you can bring it into your dining space.

PREVIOUS PAGES The saturated colours of *Asteroid City* are bleached to a haze by the blazing sun.

—

BELOW The perfectly staged world of Asteroid City combines 19th-century USA with mid-century mod cons.

—

OPPOSITE Achieve instant sunshine with desert-bright oranges and searing blues.

COLOUR PALETTE SATURATION

Edward Norton as Tennessee Williams-tribute Conrad Earp explains it at the beginning of *Asteroid City*: because this three-act play is set in the desert halfway between Parched Gulch and Arid Plains, it is unforgivingly and relentlessly lit by clean sunlight. In those sections of the film that take place in the town itself, the colours are bright and saturated, like the floor around an outdoor pool at midday in summer.

Apart from being a style device that neatly divides the black-and-white television show from the technicolor play in action, the lighting also casts an unwavering eye on the community in the desert, sending nary a cloud to relieve them and, on the more aesthetic side of things, bringing out a kaleidoscope of beautiful blues, yellows and reds. The effect is one of feeling the need to always be wearing sunglasses (or, indeed, a refracting box).

THE WILD WEST

'Life west of the Rocky Mountains' is Conrad Earp's primary playwriting fixation, meaning that the trappings of the Wild Wild West abound. Like the frontier people who pushed across the centre of the USA to reach the west coast in the 19th century, the characters in *Asteroid City* are seeking a new manifest destiny, one that involves even further exploration beyond the reaches of the universe as it was then known.

Still, the trappings of the original frontier on the other side of the Rockies can be found everywhere, their most on-the-nose appearances a pattern of cowboys, horses, lassos and cacti created by costume designer Milena Canonero for Earp's house jacket and the wallpaper of the 'twelve-stool luncheonette'. Similarly western in tone – though much more modern – are the single-pump gas station, the Stetsons, the horns on the walls of Earp's office, and countless other leitmotifs.

PROPERLY MADE

Life in 1950s America left a lot to be desired, but there's no denying that there were a lot of good things about it, too. First and foremost – and as any enthusiastic antiquer will know – furniture, cars and clothes were made splendidly well. War photographer Augie Steenbeck (Jason Schwartzman)'s car, a Mercury Monterey, may break down to serve the plot, but it sure looks terrific. So do the Chryslers, Fords and Cadillacs that pepper the screen time.

BELOW The hyper-stylized signage of 1950s commerce makes a microcosm of post-war capitalism.

—

OPPOSITE Mercurys, Chryslers, Fords and Cadillacs are among the car makes to be found in the 87-person town.

The vending machines at the motel, which also malfunction as part of the plot, are stunningly beautiful too, offering everything from parcels of land to hosiery, and from ammunition to martinis (with a twist). These – along with plenty more details mapped out by Wes, production designer Adam Stockhausen and set decorator Kris Moran – were on display as part of an exhibition in London in 2023, the year the film was released. With close-up scrutiny, they retain their almost preternatural perfection.

OTHERWORLDLY

Asteroid City is at the precipice of the rest of the universe, not only as the site of the titular asteroid impact site (modelled on Meteor Crater in Arizona), but also as the place where a very spindly, very polite alien visits. Combine this with Wes's esoteric vision and you have an otherworldly nowhere land that serves as the perfect 1950s microcosm, somewhere between *Looney Tunes*-esque cartoons, a romantic Hollywood western and the idealized mid-century town. Its disconnect comes in the toy-land perfection of its frontispieces and the anywhere-nowhere look of its surroundings; indeed, the film was not shot in the American desert, but outside Madrid, Spain, in Chinchón.

The interiors follow in kind, toeing the line between believability and wonder, with sugar cube-shaped clapboard houses, neatly printed blackboard menus and whimsical campfire arrangements barely concealed as stage sets. In this world, a luncheonette isn't only a place to buy a ¢15 slice of pie and a ¢40 milkshake, but a hyper-stylized representation of what a diner could, and perhaps should, be.

BRING ASTEROID CITY HOME

PLANT
Cacti, parlour palms or philodendrons

LIGHT FITTING
Overhead bell-shaded light

COLOUR COMBO
Red with blue

SMALL TWEAKS
Move your table closer to a window and/or a corner; add a night light or glow-in-the-dark stars; change chairs for stools

BIG PROJECTS
Build a banquette; add chrome and copper.

LET LIGHT IN

None of Wes's films are dark affairs, but *Asteroid City* is particularly, almost blindingly, bright. The principle applies well to a dining area, which, being the place where friends and family gather to share food, ought to be imbued with a sense of liveliness. If you can choose, place your table and chairs close to a window, and if you can't, invest in bright floor lamps that are just as illuminating but decidedly less harsh than your standard overhead light.

Alternatively, prioritize warmth in your light fittings. Bright orange or yellow fixtures create a cosy ambience and have the added benefit of bringing some of Wes's childlike joy to the space. Even more accurate to the film would be a night light in an astronomical shape, such as a star or planet. Perhaps your new 1950s dining space race can even prompt the return to your ceiling of those glow-in-the-dark stars that you've been looking for a reason to reuse.

OPPOSITE Pale pastels and pungent blues make this Miami sitting room, designed by architect Holborn and styled by Bettina Lafond, appear awash with bright sunlight.

MIAMI

MAKE A BANQUETTE OF YOUR SEATING

No one short of a millionaire can build a bona fide diner in their home, but you can get somewhere close to the homely communal comforts of one by incorporating a dining nook or banquette into a corner of your kitchen or as part of your dining room. A banquette is essentially an upholstered bench that clings to a wall or corner, and they're most typically found in eateries like the Luncheonette, meaning that they hold a special kind of nostalgic magic, particularly when placed in a corner to create a nook. DIY banquette projects abound on YouTube and DIY blogs, as well as the ubiquitous Ikea hack suggestions, if you want to give it a try yourself; alternatively, find a reliable tradesperson who can build one for you.

Failing the room or the resources, you could do the same as the Luncheonette – which is too narrow to be building benches – and substitute with stools. For an ordinary table try pouffe stools, or for breakfast bars and counters go full saloon with swivel bar stools. Even arranging the chairs and table you already have in a corner to imitate a nook or booth will add a touch of mid-century conviviality to the room.

BELOW Interior designer Merve Kahraman lends a contemporary take to the diner's banquette with clean wooden accents and modern artwork.

—

OPPOSITE LEFT Who says walls are for prints and paintings only? This cheerful display of ceramics by Vaisselle Boutique (@Vaisselle.boutique), photographed by Hana Snow (@hana.snow), proves the value of thinking outside the box.

—

OPPOSITE RIGHT Esther's (@el_loves_colour) bold Melbourne kitchen is directly inspired by American canteens and diners, complete with 1950s-coded Smeg fridge.

DECK THE WALLS

How many traditional diners have you been to that are bereft of decorations like huge menus, framed pictures, posters and even flags? Likely, you answered 'none'. The Luncheonette plumps for a wall-dominating blackboard menu and a Wild West wallpaper, but other diners of the 1950s – which Anderson and Stockhausen consulted for their own design – are even more thorough in their decoration, with framed pictures of cult figures, gaudy mirrors, public service signs, plaques and neon signs hoisted on to their walls.

You might not have thought to bring your gallery wall skills into the dining room, or above your dining area, but the effect can be transformative, bringing a level of lived-in care to your own space that loving establishment owners hope to convey to their customers. You could recreate a poster, picture and painting extravaganza (see pages 40–1), or you could get more creative with your mediums by introducing collectible crockery, branded mirrors, registration plates, hand-painted murals and other features typical of the quintessential diner. While the effect in some more down-at-heel establishments can be decidedly harsh, a collage like this will look subtle and beautiful so long as you stick to a unifying colour theme. Pastels look most Wes, but other palettes including red with pink, dark blue with purple, or buttermilk-yellow and grass-green, would also look terrific.

KINDNESS IS THE NEW ROCK AND ROLL
oasis
Band on the Run
romance
Andy Warhol
God Games
the
The

CHROME AND COPPER

Shining, polished surfaces with metal trim were the bold lifeblood of 1950s Americana: cars, eateries, rockets...so a healthy helping of such materials will bring the same kind of impressive pride to your space. Chrome suits cooler colour palettes best, while copper is best placed in warmer surroundings. Both look at home in the dining and kitchen spaces in a way that they might not in a cosier space, such as a lounge or bedroom. Introduce them through pin legs or flourishes on chairs, light fittings and even table accessories, such as salt and pepper shakers.

OPPOSITE Emma Jane Palin uses record sleeves as the artwork for her dining gallery wall. She adds a mid-century American kick with an outsized copper bubble light.

—

RIGHT Communal eating in non-traditional dining spaces – such as a breakfast bar in a kitchen – have the effect of the Luncheonette.

ASTEROID CITY IN OTHER ROOMS

The patio

If you live somewhere warm, or exist for the fleeting weeks in which the place you reside welcomes summer, then an outdoor space like a patio, balcony or even windowsill is very important – for design purposes and for a sense of wellbeing. A pasting of bright blue on a sun umbrella, garden table or windowsill evokes the pure, endless sky of the American West, while a dash of gingham – whether on a tablecloth or a flag to plant in a pot – offers both an interesting colour contrast and a more obvious Americana flair. Larger spaces could incorporate the white picket fence effect of bright trellising (and perhaps a white picket fence itself); smaller spaces could drop in preppy stripes or gingham, perhaps in the form of planters or outdoor seating. At least one cactus, of any size, is a must.

OPPOSITE Cacti, gingham, fairy lights and striped awnings are all part and parcel of the constructed outdoor American experience.

—

ABOVE Curtains in the bathroom needn't only surround the shower. How about a privacy stand and a pair of twee nylon drapes at the window?

The bathroom

The only view we get into Midge Campbell (Scarlett Johansson)'s rented bathroom is through the postage-stamp window facing Schwartzman's Augie, yet we're more than spoiled for design inspiration. Within, we're treated to a view of a mint-green and lemon-yellow tiled floor (colours that imitate the stripes on the hallways in *The Life Aquatic*) with a matching bathtub. Changing one's bath and floor is not a weekend job. Seeking a charming, vintage-inspired shower curtain, however, is. The motel bathroom's curtain is a diaphanous cream affair, but take inspiration, too, from the colourful flowers on the curtain on the room's privacy stand. If you have a glass panel around your shower, consider installing a curtain rail somewhere else: between the toilet and the sink, for example, or in the corner you tend to dry off in.

HOST AN ASTEROID CITY DINNER PARTY

Like most of the country's touchpoints, the USA's foodstuff is implicitly understood. Chilli and hot dogs, burgers, ice-cream floats and sodas all feel particularly American, and they also smack of block parties from mid-century to the present day. You'll play rock 'n' roll, folk and rockabilly, and play games – purists will rent a jukebox for the occasion and instigate a name game. Perhaps you could even set off fireworks. Invitations beg for either the style of a Junior Stargazers' award (Collapsing Star Ribbon of Success, Red Giant Sash of Honour, and so on) or the comic book-like punchiness of the titular town's 'Regional Monument' billboard, complete with a bright illustration of the crater and your menu in a mid-century font.

SUGGESTED DISHES

MAIN
Chilli and hot dogs with ketchup, mustard, relish and onions

SIDES
Corn on the cob, milkshake

DESSERT
Gooseberry ice cream

TABLESCAPE

Pretend you're at a Fourth of July party in 1955 with a red gingham tablecloth, and have the ketchup, mustard and mayo proudly out on the table (instructions on how to make a caddy on pages 156–7). Paper plates are fine considering this is a rustic suburban American dine-out, but if you'd rather imitate the design of the Luncheonette, swap them for plain white plates or mismatched pieces that your family have had for generations. You're going to be having milkshakes, so place straws in a glass on the table, too, and a stack of napkins for when the inevitable spillages occur.

PLAYLIST

— **Elizabeth Cotten**, 'Freight Train'
— **R L Burnside**, 'Someday Baby'
— **The Marshall Tucker Band**, 'Ab's Song'
— **Marty Robbins**, 'Big Iron'
— **Creedence Clearwater Revival**, 'Fortunate Son'
— **The Mamas & the Papas**, 'California Dreamin''
— **Big Mama Thornton**, 'Hound Dog'
— **Fats Domino**, 'Ain't That a Shame'

ASTRONOMICAL ELLIPSES

Anyone who drinks alcohol and has seen *Asteroid City* will wish that the martini vending machine really exists, and while it sadly doesn't, you can make a concoction by hand that might taste better than anything a machine could cook up. The Astronomical Ellipses is a twist on the French martini with three ingredients (plus ice and garnish).

— 40ml (1¼US fl.oz) vodka
— 20ml (¾US fl.oz) Chambord
— 80ml 2¾US floz) mango juice
— Ice
— Lemon peel

Shake the ingredients together over ice. Strain and add lemon peel to serve.

DREAM GUEST LIST

— Cleopatra
— Jagadish Chandra Bose
— Antonie van Leeuwenhoek
— Paracelsus
— Kurt Gödel
— William Henry Bragg
— Lord Kelvin
— Konstantin Tsiolkovsky

HOW TO MAKE A DINER CONDIMENT BOX

YOU WILL NEED

Materials

Wood (any kind, ideally 18mm/¾in thick)
Plywood (ideally 6mm/¼in thick, for base)
Wood glue
Wood screws
Panel pins
Felt
Contact adhesive
18mm/¾in dowel

Tools

Dust mask, ear protectors and eye protection
Hand saw
Tape measure/rule square
Clamps
Plate sander (60- and 120-grit sanding pads)
Drill (3mm/⅛in and 18mm/¾in/countersink wood bits)
Phillips head screwdriver

1. Using a hand saw, cut two wooden side panels to size (95mm/3¾in x 190mm/7½in), making sure the edges are square.
2. Mark out dimensions for the end panels, which should taper to a tented top. Maximum height 170mm (6¾in), 40mm (1½in) along the top edge and 110mm (4⅓in) height at the junction to the side panels. Secure with clamps and cut using a hand saw.
3. Drill an 18mm (¾in) hole in the centre of the two end pieces, about 30mm (1¼in) from the top. Take care to drill from both sides part way to avoid the wood splintering.
4. Align the side and end pieces and mark the position for three screws at the top, middle and bottom. Drill 3mm (⅛in) pilot holes in each marked screw position and countersink.
5. Select appropriate wood screws and wood glue in readiness for connecting the four panels.
6. Sand all pieces using first 60- and then 120-grit sandpaper.
7. Apply wood glue to the edges of the end panels following the manufacturer's guidelines, then screw the side panels to each corner.
8. Place the joined upper section over the piece of plywood and draw a pencil line around the outside perimeter to measure the base, then cut to size using a hand saw.
9. Tack the plywood base to the underside of the upper section with panel pins, then cover the base with felt using contact adhesive.
10. Measure the distance from the outside edge of one end panel to the outside edge of the other and cut a piece of 18mm (¾in) wooden dowel to this length. Push fit the length of dowel into the two holes to fit flush at both ends.

Nautical Mediterranean

The LIFE AQUATIC

THE BATHROOM

Part 7

For *The Life Aquatic with Steve Zissou*, Wes Anderson and his team of model makers, production designers and carpenters created a 12m (40ft) tall, 46m (150ft)-long cross-section of a boat named the *Belafonte*. In the context of the film, it's a long-range sub-hunter turned documentarian's lair inhabited by the morose Steve Zissou and his crew of Lost Boys. In reality, it is a doll's house in the cinematic playroom of Wes Anderson. The fantasy? A nostalgic picture of a nautical, Mediterranean-cum-French mess hall on the ocean.

A NOD TO NAUTICAL

So many real-life examples of the nautical style are mired in ugly lengths of obsolete rope, ornamental seagulls and clinical, blue-painted wood, but in *The Life Aquatic*, Anderson proves that there is a much chicer way to work with maritime themes. In his vision, the world of Steve Zissou is more whimsical summer retreat than sad beach house. Notes of ocean life and oceanside dwellings abound everywhere on both the *Belafonte* and the Pescespada island base, weaving together a mishmash of Southern European influences. Thus, Anderson constructs a home aquatic, giving us a playbook on how to decorate the bathroom.

PREVIOUS PAGES Bill Murray as Steve Zissou is a fictional recreation of Jacques Cousteau, complete with iconic pale blue shirt and red beanie hat.

—

BELOW A behind-the-scenes view of the 46m (150ft) *Belafonte* complete with helicopter and submarine.

—

OPPOSITE True to the nautical inspiration and setting of the film, sea-blues dominate the colour palette, with warm browns and pops of red to offset.

COLOUR PALETTE OCEANIC INFLUENCE

Jacques Cousteau, the French naval officer, oceanographer and filmmaker who inspired the character of Steve Zissou, once said that he was 'miserable out of the water'. Bill Murray's fictional estimation shares that melancholy, and the places he inhabits prove his need to be close to the ocean. Pet killer whale aside, there are innumerable maritime references, from seafaring maps on the walls to tank-side tiles framing windows. The peeling aquamarine walls of the island compound aren't only a direct reference to the colours found in Italian and Greek towns, but imitate the shades of the ocean, too.

Blue continues inside the compound, but in a subtler way than one might expect: paired with yellow and green in a series of painted stripes and as feature walls beside beige ones.

On the boat, the notes of the briny deep are eminently more recognizable: windows are portholes, doors are surrounded by rivets and stairs are ladders. Though all these things are essential to the infrastructure of the ship, they offer more than just context; they are quirks that make this space, which seems so much like a home, feel almost otherworldly.

RIGHT The blue-tiled sauna of the *Belafonte* is as nostalgic to look at as the chlorine in a swimming pool is to smell.

—

OPPOSITE Groundbreaking underwater explorer and inventor of the aqualung, Jacques-Yves Cousteau, who served as Anderson's inspiration for Steve Zissou.

SUMMER CAMP

The film's production designer, Mark Friedberg, aimed at 'somewhere between a science facility and a summer camp' with the creation of the spaces in *The Life Aquatic*, hoping to bring out the passion of team Zissou, while emphasizing their Peter Pan-like need to stay forever young. He succeeded; both the Zissou compound and the *Belafonte* have the echoing, ramshackle feel of the facilities that children holiday in with such institutions as the Scouts. Carpets are in scarce supply and tile is king; lighting is just as likely to be a desk lamp or a model of the sun as it is a simple table lamp; beds are utilitarian; the observation bubble looks more like a den than anything else.

Everywhere you find reminders of the crew's childlike existence, though there is evidence of grown-up choices, too. The kitchen is light on cupboards but bursting with wine racks like student accommodation...yet the research library is a cerebral space of serious dark woods. An ex-wife's name is unceremoniously crossed off the mini sub rather than painted over...yet the mess hall is clean and uncluttered. Nowhere is this feeling of dichotomy truer than in the sauna, which was designed by an 'engineer from the Chinese space programme' and has a Swedish masseuse on staff...but in all its blue tile and curved lines looks as though it smells of the chlorine of a kids' pool.

MEDITERRANEAN-FRENCH

The Life Aquatic is an American movie inspired by the life of Frenchman Jacques Cousteau and filmed in Italy. This international mash-up is a magical one – at once anachronistic and disorientating with, to name one visual representation, its varsity stripes abutting European lacquered wood. The effect is one of seeing into a fabled world that thrives on adventure and has visited every corner of the Earth. Even though there is a dearth of curios on the ship, wanderlust is implied in other ways; wandering animals in the compound, the occasional wall map and a varied assortment of interior styles all convey the worldliness of this environment and the crew who live in it.

That same romantic, hazy American view of a homogenized 'Europe' appears in the frescoed halls in which Zissou's films are premiered, the hotel bar Steve and son Ned (Owen Wilson) share wine in, and Jeff Goldblum-as-Captain Hennessey's coastal home. By contrast, Hennessey's boat is clinical, expensive-looking and Americanized, with lashings of chrome and steel that make it almost NASA-like. The suaver seaman may have enviable equipment, but it's obvious that Anderson's aesthetic loyalties lie with the crumblier European kind.

BRING THE LIFE AQUATIC HOME

PLANT
Olive tree

LIGHT FITTING
Novelty space-themed lamps or wall-mounted shell lights

COLOUR COMBO
Red with blue

SMALL TWEAKS
A round bathmat; stick-and-peel tile border; thrifted ceramic animals; a vase of flowers; hanging framed maps; drapes around the bathtub

BIG PROJECTS
A multi-patterned retiling; arches and tiled columns; ornate framed mirrors; round windows.

TILE EVERYTHING

Mosaic, terracotta, hexagonal, decorative and glass brick: the bathroom's function dictates that it must be made of tile and glass, but that doesn't mean you don't have options in colour, pattern and even shape. The hallways of the Zissou compound are a wonderful example of how several of these things can work harmoniously in one space.

Chequerboard floors are traditional, but you can add the flavour of Anderson's vintage leanings with colours other than black and white, or choose a patterned design for even more foundational interest. Contrast the walls with a different shaped tile. If you can't do up a whole bathroom in this way, you could choose an interesting splashback for your sink, or add a border of peel-and-stick tiles around the walls, roughly halfway up.

Another option for a quick switch-up without the hassle of getting in the builders is painting your own tiles. While it might sound like a big job, paint companies now have an impressive range of specialist paints that make bringing some Anderson bright to your space easy. You can either paint plain colours or choose a stencil design to add pattern – retailers such as Etsy offer a range of stencil designs that can be made to your exact tile size.

OPPOSITE Blue tiles of different sizes on the floor and walls of this retro bathroom provide the swimming-pool chic aesthetic as captured by Anderson in the *Belafonte* sauna.

ODDITIES ARE FOR BATHROOMS, TOO

No one, not even Jacques Cousteau, can keep an orca as a pet, but you could find a vintage ornament of one to place on the windowsill. It doesn't have to be an orca, of course. So long as you shirk the mass-produced seagull statues seen in so many ugly nautical bathrooms, you could add any critter you like. Most antiques shops and vintage stores carry ornamental doodahs, plenty of which come in the preferable materials of bone china or ceramic. Frequently found pieces include jumping dolphins to make a quirky addition to shelving, and seated leopards to bring some interest to the corners of rooms.

Oddities can come in other forms: a ceramic light pull in the shape of a cute critter; a battery-powered night light in the shape of a tin of sardines; a pair of goggles hung from the wall; a bright, patterned or transparent shower curtain; even the simplest touch, such as a vase of flowers in the bathroom, is totally different. And remember: if it's unexpected, it will carry the energy of Anderson's *The Life Aquatic*.

OPPOSITE Wood panelling and antique etchings make this bathroom look for all the world like a 19th-century sea captain's.

—

RIGHT Framed pictures add instant warmth and interest to a bathroom.

ADD FRAMED PICTURES

It's the room where you're least likely to find a hanging print, but if you have a wall left without tile at the end of your renovation then add one. Keep in mind that condensation may wrinkle the paper inside the frame, so don't hang anything treasured. Rather, choose maps or graphs found in the ephemera section of an antiques shop, or reprints of photos featuring your loved ones on holiday. As with any Wes Anderson project, colour is better than monochrome, and ornate frames are better than plain ones. For something less literal and more thematic, a framed painting or mirror of any kind will add a vintage, eccentric touch.

LEFT A unique pillar sink and curved tap introduces interesting shapes to Emma Jane Palin's retro bathroom.

—

RIGHT A round window brings visual interest to the bathroom as well as referencing portholes found on boats.

THROW SOME SHAPES

Like a great outfit, a room fulfils its potential when it is interesting in colour and/or texture and/or shape. You rarely find the last in bathrooms, which tend to be square and functional in their lines and angles, and that's why fans of esoteric design gravitate towards vintage spaces that have tiled archways over walk-in showers or baths. Adding structural shape to an existing room is a bigger project, involving fundamental reworking or clever DIY. If you do end up adding an arch, it'll look even smarter with a contrasting tiled frame or different colours of tile inside and outside the portal. Other big projects include adding round windows (like a large porthole) or unusually shaped storage alcoves in the shower. There are pillar-like curves in the Zissou compound hallways (tiled, natch) that would look amazing in the corners or middle of your walls, too.

To get the look without changing the infrastructure of your bathroom, introduce a curved section of tile that references the sweeping lines of the *Belafonte* sauna (for extra-easy points, you could do this with tile paint), or hang draped curtains in front of the bathtub. Even adding a rounded bathmat or unusually shaped mirror will add some of this gravitas.

THE LIFE AQUATIC IN OTHER ROOMS

LEFT Bill Murray peers through a porthole on the set of *The Life Aquatic*.

—

OPPOSITE Owen Wilson as Ned Plimpton and Willem Dafoe as Klaus Daimler face off in a hallway of wood and faded blue paint.

The office

The *Belafonte*'s study is a serious space in the context of the otherwise cartoonishly adolescent boat. With dark woods and cloth-bound books aplenty, the only hints that it belongs on the sea are the slightly tilted floor and closed porthole, but that doesn't mean it isn't a place we can take inspiration from. Wes canon seems to advocate for original shop fittings as cabinetry (more on that on page 98), a chintzy armchair and soft lighting in the form of green glass notary lamps. The easiest tweak to steal from this brief shot of the study? Organize your books by colour, to create a rainbow of spines neatly arranged on the shelves.

The hallways

Among the film's strongest suggestions of the Zissou compound as a camp are the echoing hallways of the Pescespada island base. I've already mentioned the collegiate stripes that add a sporty alternative to a dado rail, but note, too, how furniture for storage spills out into these corridors. Lacking space in one of your rooms? Even if it's a squeeze, a dark wood chest of drawers in the hall will add an interesting, almost eccentric element to your home. In addition to the practical storage, you can also use it as the foundation for further visual interest. Team Zissou keep a reel-to-reel tape recorder on top of theirs, but think of it as another place for your collection of antique and charity-shop ornaments, a vintage dresser doily or a place to keep your important correspondence in a fun receptacle (for instructions on how to make your own indoor 'mailbox', see pages 132–3).

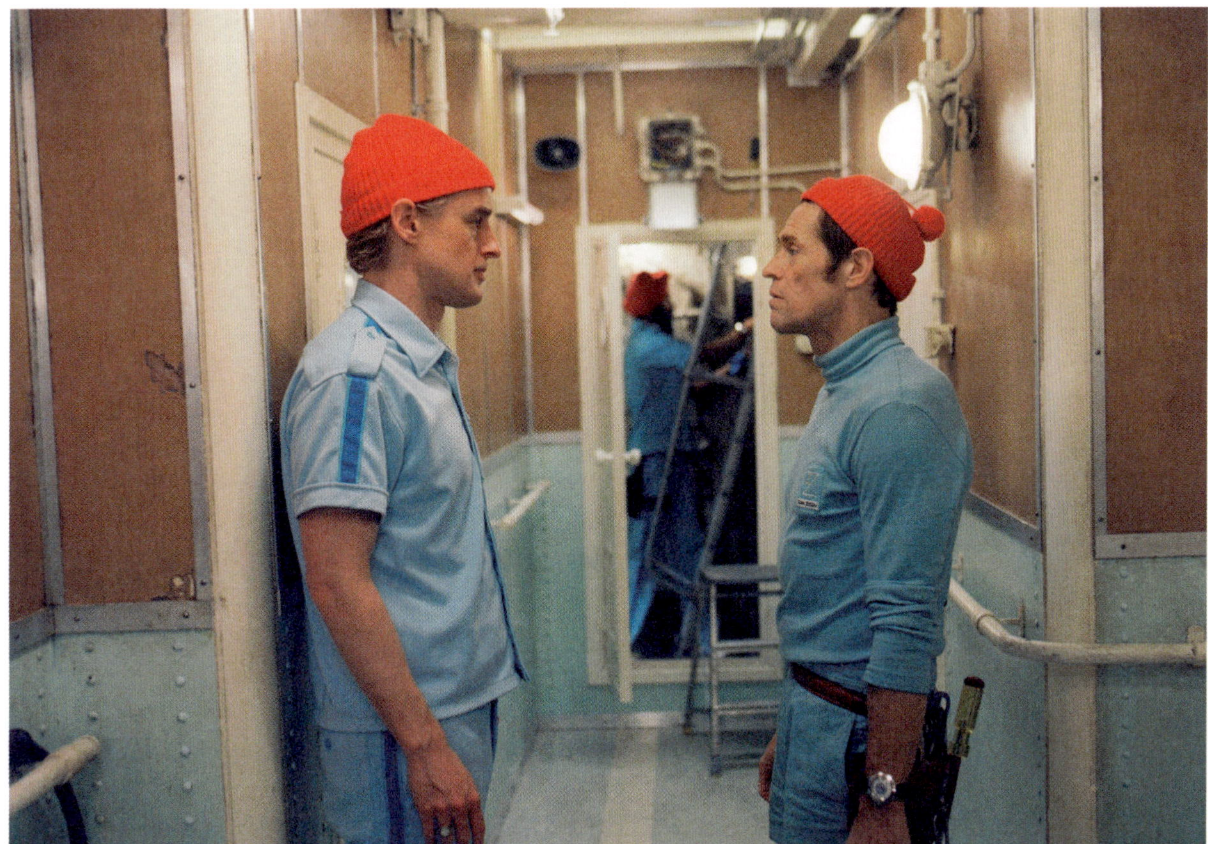

HOST A LIFE AQUATIC LUNCHEON

A lot more cigarette smoking goes on in *The Life Aquatic* than eating and drinking, but we do see the crew feasting on lobsters, salad and bread with a magnum of Moët et Chandon champagne as they discuss mutiny. We also get two key insights into Steve Zissou's eating habits: the first is that his favourite food is sardines, and the second that he partakes in a Campari every once in a while. Fish and bitter booze? Just the ticket for a depressed mariner.

A *Life Aquatic* luncheon will be a spread of Mediterranean/French and pescatarian staples with a focus on freshness, because who would have fresher fish than the crew of a ship? Go to a fishmonger for your sardines (or other choice, such as sea bass) and shellfish, and buy in some fizz to go with your cocktail. Moët is screen accurate, but since characters in *The Fantastic Mr. Fox* drink Dom Perignon and characters in *The Grand Budapest Hotel* Perrier Jouët, it doesn't seem that Mr Anderson is too picky about his champagne brands. Nor should you be.

SUGGESTED DISHES

MAIN
Grilled or BBQ sardines and lobster

SIDES
Greek salad and French bread

DESSERT
French apple tart

TABLESCAPE

The mess-hall tables on the *Belafonte* are simple wood or Formica with no trimmings, but that doesn't mean you can't have fun with yours. Serve your condiments (tartare sauce or salsa verde, most likely) in hollowed-out oyster and clam shells, and your chocolate favours in miniature beanie hats (see pages 178–9). If you have access to a crystal ship's decanter then present your cocktail mix in one of those, and laminate nautical charts and/or chequerboards for place mats.

PLAYLIST

— **David Bowie**, 'Life on Mars'
— **Joan Baez**, 'Diamonds and Rust'
— **Iggy Pop**, 'Search and Destroy'
— **Bob Dylan**, 'Blowin' in the Wind'
— **Gang of Four**, 'Damaged Goods'
— **Charlotte Gainsbourg**, 'Ring-a-Ring O'Roses'
— **Wunderhorse**, 'Aeroplane'
— **Nick Cave & the Bad Seeds**, 'O Children'
— **Townes Van Zandt**, 'Waiting Around to Die'
— **Ramones**, 'I Wanna Be Sedated'

NEGRONI SBAGLIATO

A grumpy man with European persuasions could only gravitate to a bitter classic like the negroni. Make it a sbagliato and substitute champagne for prosecco to make this an even more sophisticated tipple.

— 30ml (1US fl.oz) Campari
— 30ml (1 US fl.oz) Vermouth
— 50ml (1¾ US fl.oz) champagne

Gently mix the Campari and vermouth with ice and top up with champagne.

DREAM GUEST LIST

— Jacques-Yves Cousteau and Simone Melchior Cousteau
— Sir David Attenborough
— Steve Irwin
— David Bowie
— Rachel Carson
— Ocean Ramsey

HOW TO MAKE KNITTED BEANIE TABLE FAVOURS

Wes Anderson's vision of Zissou's wardrobe is remarkably similar to that of Cousteau: lots of baby blues with a contrasting knit beanie cap. It is this knit cap that is the enduring symbol of *The Life Aquatic*, which is why it should feature somehow in any themed parties you throw. In this project, find instructions on how to knit your own series of miniature beanies that will fit perfectly over a chocolate bon-bon and can be offered on every party attendee's table place. Alternatively, triple the amount of wool for a hat that will fit over a typical bath bomb.

YOU WILL NEED

Pair of 4mm knitting needles (UK size 8, US size 6)
Red double-knit yarn
Darning needle

1. Cast on 30 stitches.
2. Work 3 rows in rib stitch (knit 1, purl 1).
3. Next row (purl 1, purl 2 together) to end = 20 stitches.
4. Knit 10 rows of stocking stitch (alternating rows of knit and purl), beginning with a knit row.
5. Next row (knit 2, knit 2 together) to end = 15 stitches.
6. Purl 1 row.
7. Next row (knit 1, knit 2 together) to end = 10 stitches.
8. Purl 1 row.
9. Break off the yarn and thread through the remaining stitches. Pull tight.
10. Oversew the two ends of the hat together.

Dopamine Decor

The GRAND BUDAPEST HOTEL

The Bedroom

Part 8

All Wes Anderson's films are a feast for the eyes, but with its kaleidoscope of colours, perfect symmetry and lovingly dressed period sets, *The Grand Budapest Hotel* is a banquet. A favourite of even casual film fans, almost every frame of this emotional, dramatic, comedic and aesthetic masterpiece is ripe for vision boards. There may be lashings of that classic Anderson melancholy within the story, but the interior design – particularly that of the hotel's 1930s heyday – makes you nothing short of giddy. For this reason, it's a blue (pink?) print for dopamine decor.

DOSE UP THE DOPAMINE

Popping colours, daring clashes and antique patinas abound in the world of Ralph Fiennes's vain, cultured and liberally perfumed M. Gustave, opening up possibilities for indoor landscapes that you'd probably never considered in your wildest dreams...and that's just the lift. The intricacy and volume of the sets – both life-size, in the case of the hotel's interior, and miniature, in the case of the exterior – are responsible for a healthy portion of Anderson-indebted interiors, giving the go-ahead on using four different colours in one room or deploying an unlimited number of crisscrossing patterns. The fictional hotel also serves as one of the best and most recognizable examples of Art Nouveau in modern culture.

PREVIOUS PAGES The intricately detailed model of *The Grand Budapest Hotel* used in filming is 2.7m (9ft) tall, 4.2m (14ft) long and 2m (7ft) deep.

—

BELOW Ralph Fiennes as M. Gustave stands in front of the specially created concierge desk. The cubbyholes in which the keys hang can still be found in many hotels today, including the Hotel El Palace in Barcelona, Spain.

—

OPPOSITE The surprising combination of purple and red cuts through the washes of pink in *The Grand Budapest Hotel*.

COLOUR PALETTE
DOPAMINE DRENCHING

The colour, the texture, the attention to detail, the quality of crafts, the needless fussiness: all these things go some way towards making those shots of *The Grand Budapest Hotel* so indulgent. Every corner of the building has been lovingly attended to and decorated, and it is this care and attention that make it a prime example of dopamine decor.

A storied aesthetic with a 21st-century update and a new name courtesy of the TikTok generation, 'dopamine decor' is an interior design trend that embraces bright and interesting colours, patterns, textures and playful details, all chosen to maximize feel-good vibes.

The basic philosophy is: decorate according to what you love. Just as in a Wes Anderson set, every corner of a dopamine home is carefully considered. And nowhere is this more obvious than in the colour choices. Anderson's film is a confection of reds and pinks accented with bright blues and royal purple.

IMPECCABLE QUALITY

It's telling that the hotel of the prologue – the mid-century modern establishment of 1968 – looks just as well made as its glorious 1930s forebear. Though the Brutalist outer shell, mustard Formica and low ceiling say a lot about the hard (and Soviet) times the hotel has fallen on, you can tell that Anderson couldn't help but source only the very best for every scene.

It's a recognizable trope of Anderson's. An antidote to CGI, his films instead champion handmade worlds that feel as much like exhibitions of crafts as they do Hollywood movies. Nowhere is this truer than on the set of *The Grand Budapest Hotel*, which drafted in large teams with jobs as specific as drapesmaster, milliner and Klimt forger to deploy filmmaking tricks including puppetry, model making, sleight of hand and hand-picked props. In the last category, experts in antiques sourced furnishings from various spots around Europe, as well as contemporaneous pieces made specifically for the film. Old or new, only the best was used. Just two of the many modern artisans credited include Parisian fashion house Olympia Le-Tan, which embroidered the 'part 4' handkerchief, and German bakery Anemone Müller-Großmann, which created the three-tiered profiterole patisserie Mendl's Courtesan au Chocolat.

ABOVE Graphic designer Annie Atkins misspelled 'patisserie' on the thousands of boxes she and her team handmade for the film; each had to be altered in post-production.

—

OPPOSITE The glass entranceway to the hotel references the Parisian Métro signage first imagined by Hector Guimard in 1900.

DOORWAY TO FANTASIA

Each and every archway and door of *The Grand Budapest Hotel* is a portal to a new world of lustrous decoration. The arch to the funicular is frosted with pastel cartouches reminiscent of the sugary creations of Mendl's, the hotel-room doors are painted sunshine-yellow, and there are both square and curved archways in the halls and the lobby of the hotel. Even the entranceways to the smaller sets – the prison, the Lutz cemetery, Madame D's mansion – are detailed art projects with lovingly crafted borders. These casings present each set as a piece of art, and the entryways that appear as ornate frames are integral to showing off the creativity and beauty created within each building and room.

SHRINE TO ART NOUVEAU

Selected by production designer Adam Stockhausen and dressed by set decorator Anna Pinnock, the lobby of *The Grand Budapest Hotel* is actually the main atrium of the Art Nouveau building and former department store Görlitzer Warenhaus on the German-Polish border. As such, there are pieces of this vast space that exist independently of Wes Anderson's fantasy world: the delicately ornate panes of the vaulted glass ceiling, the superfluous columns, the marble-effect stone foundation, the patterned tiles, the crystal chandeliers and the unique staircase bridge.

Elsewhere, Anderson and his team took cues from old-world Europe, adding pink and yellow paint, palms, globe lights, a fine circular desk and an ocean of oriental rugs. The main doorway is crowned by a spray of cast iron and the hotel name in a curly font, both of which reference the distinctive entranceways to the Parisian Métro. In short, the vision of this hotel is a joint venture between the original architects of the Görlitzer Warenhaus, Anderson's team of set dressers and production designers, and the many artisans who, over the years, lovingly created every prop sourced for the film.

BELOW The interior of the Görlitzer Warenhaus before it was dressed by Anderson and his production designers.

—

OPPOSITE The shade of red in the lacquered elevator is echoed on the trim of the hotel staff's lapels, a surprising, and very Anderson, contrast to the bright purple.

PROUDLY PEACOCKING

From the first shot of the sugary building perched on the mountainside, it's clear that the titular hotel is proud of its elaborate looks. Symmetrical turrets, doll's-house-pink walls and an Art Nouveau entrance make an architectural peacock of the building's model, as richly detailed in its funicular as it is in its turreted roof. Columns, marbled stonework, Métro-style frills: everything about the 1930s hotel exudes an opulence that only a select few five-star establishments share today. In its glass-topped atrium alone, the Grand Budapest Hotel is the most jaw-dropping feat of leisure architecture that never existed.

The glimpses we get of the other parts of the hotel in its heyday are equally debonair, from the plushly carpeted, wood-panelled bedrooms to the lavender-hued tiled bathhouse. It's convincing, is it not, that the rich, old, insecure, vain, superficial, blonde and needy ladies M. Gustave entertains would gravitate here season after season?

BRING THE GRAND BUDAPEST HOTEL HOME

PLANT
Palms of all kinds: kentia and sago palms most closely match those used in the film.

LIGHT FITTING
Globular pendant lights hung in bunches or at regular intervals; exposed bulbs around an archway.

COLOUR COMBO
Pink with red; yellow with purple

SMALL TWEAKS
Curved door and cupboard handles; oval rugs; an oriental rug in place of a bathmat; swap grey and beige for sorbet shades.

BIG PROJECTS
Scalloped glass canopies or partitions; archways; a sea of colourful rugs; curled flourishes to paint, picture rails and dado rails; a circular bed in plush velvet.

ANY COLOUR GOES

Dopamine decor involves a lot of colour. A total rejection of the 'sad beige' aesthetic popularized by the Kardashian family in the 2010s, this movement instead insists upon a more imaginative palette. In *The Grand Budapest Hotel*, that means lots of reds and pinks with soft washes of yellow and – through the concierge team's uniforms – shocks of purple. The rich browns, bright oranges and lacquered yellows of the hotel in the 1960s also work well for those who share Anderson's love of mid-century modern design, but – as per the rules of dopamine decor – so long as you like them together, any colours go: pink with pistachio-green, red with sky-blue, and buttermilk-yellow with mauve. Can't paint your walls or doors? Introduce these colours through rugs, headboards, lampshades and curtains instead.

OPPOSITE Hanna's (@hanna.k.l) Swedish apartment in Gothenburg makes stunningly beautiful use of red, pink and blue.

ADD WHAT YOU LOVE

So long as it makes you smile, almost anything goes with dopamine decor. While that does often mean a splash of colour, modern interpretations of the style also include plenty of plants and flowers, interesting or unusual lighting (including neon), eclectic choices in mirrors and wall hangings, and clashing patterns.

There are plenty of rugs, sofas, lamps and so on that offer these colours and patterns built in, but you could also mix and match textures, colours and prints manually, such as with two or more comparable but differently patterned ornate rugs (like the red ones found in the film), or with a yellow blind and a pink set of curtains. For the Art Nouveau thrust of the film, look for porcelain flowers (as ornaments or a unique lampshade, as shown here), rich textures (such as velvet in curtains or cushions, or wicker in bed frames or armchairs) and delicacy (primarily in engraving and ornate mouldings).

ABOVE Touches of Art Nouveau are achieved through the curved mirror frame, gilded cushion and artwork in this bedroom.

—

OPPOSITE LEFT Esther of @el_loves_colour upcycled this dressing table and painted it in butter-yellow for her walk-in wardrobe. A curved mirror, pink wall and foliage add to the Art Deco effect.

—

OPPOSITE RIGHT Sandra's (@the_idle_hands) bedroom makes expert work of clashing prints, made especially effective with that sweeping, curved headboard.

REJECT RIGIDITY IN FAVOUR OF FLUID LINES

A central tenet of the Art Nouveau movement was to reject the rigidity of the 19th century in favour of more ornate and flowery styles. From Gustav Klimt's gold-leaf paintings to Otto Eckmann's florid, medieval-inspired typeface to stained-glass Tiffany lamps: the admiration of nature in all its forms can be found in Art Nouveau (which would have been called 'Jugendstil' in the fictional Germanic country of Zubrowka, where the hotel is set).

Honouring the style in your bedroom should mean a distinct move away from the sharp lines that characterize modern buildings. Instead of hard right angles, introduce sinuous lines: on walls that could come via the medium of undulating paint or wallpaper; on the floors, circular rugs or rectangular ones with rounded edges. Picture and dado rails, an indicator of a period home, should be added to walls that don't have them, and added to with decorative trims and mouldings for those that do. The rails themselves, as well as the scalloped additions, can be found in stick-on iterations or in MDF form ready to be painted. If you're building a room anew, you could make the picture and dado rails undulate or break off in subtle curls that mimic shoots and leaves. Even a curved door handle in brass will add softness to the room. In short, embrace ovals and rounded edges at every opportunity.

GLASS IS GOD

The vaulted atrium of the lobby is the largest example of glass in the film, but there are innumerable examples of the material and its many intricate idiosyncrasies that characterize the film. If you have the funds, add stained glass to a windowpane or two, or in the form of Tiffany lamps at each bedside – matching, of course. You could add a touch of scalloped glass through light fittings that bookend the bed, or even as a canopy above a vanity table in dedication to the details seen in the Parisian Métro and the front entrance of the Grand Budapest Hotel.

If you'd prefer a more modern (and cheaper) immersion in this aesthetic, you could skip Art Nouveau Tiffany lamps for bubble-style lighting in shapes like clouds or stars, or have a personalized neon sign made for the wall. Cut-glass bowls and glassware also bring a fine, beautifully made element on a smaller scale.

BELOW If you aren't lucky enough to have an original feature, such as this Venetian doorway, just one panel of stained glass above a door adds an instant touch of magic. There is also stained glass window film available for an affordable (and renter-friendly) alternative.

ABOVE LEFT A demonstration from Sandra Baker (@the_idle_hands) of how you can practise the Art Deco style of *The Grand Budapest Hotel* with a subtler colour palette.

—

ABOVE RIGHT Divine Savage's Deco Martini wallpaper in blush is the perfect Art Deco backdrop for this sumptuous bedroom.

BRING THE OUTSIDE IN

You will have spotted that the reds, pinks, yellows and purples of *The Grand Budapest Hotel* are further set off by sprays of green palms and fountains of blush peonies. Against colourful rugs or wallpaper – particularly red examples – these living ornaments will look magnificent…but there are more figurative ways of incorporating plants, flowers and the wider natural world in your interiors. As a modern-day nod to the natural quirks of Art Nouveau, introduce rugs in the shape of daisies, lamps that appear to hover like clouds, and paintings or prints that depict natural scenes.

As mentioned, you can add your own palm to the room for an instant injection of *Grand Budapest* style. Even for the less green-fingered among us, palms are generally easy to care for and – as a bonus – purify the air. Alternatively, faux plants are a simple solution to add a touch of greenery.

A TEXTURED BED

In just the makeup of your bed, you can introduce a cinematic world of interest. If you aren't in a position to do up your entire bedroom, you could instead choose a vintage velvet or textile headboard with a point of interest, such as a pattern or buttons, select cotton or (for extra texture) linen bedding in a rich, contrasting colour, then add cushions in yet another colour and pattern. The more flourishes the better: tassels on cushions, frills on pillowcases, patterns on headboards and linens. Finally, add a throw to the bottom of the bed. In terms of texture, colour and pattern? You know what to do.

THE GRAND BUDAPEST HOTEL IN OTHER ROOMS

The bathroom

The Grand Budapest Hotel's bathhouse set was a case of serendipity; an abandoned one was discovered just a short walk from the Görlitzer Warenhaus, which provided the shell of the hotel lobby. We see the bathhouse most prominently during the 1960s prologue, and though it was by then in decline, a fresh version of the blue-and-white tiles and matching blue bath would look beautiful. Prefer the glimpses of the 1930s baths? Try painting pastel flowers on the walls or ceilings, adding wicker or rattan (in the form of a laundry basket, armchair or shelving unit), and introducing palms. The most radical but relatively easy tweak you could make is to add a Persian rug in place of a bathmat.

The hallway

Think of the first interior glance of your house – whether it be a short corridor into a flat, a porch or a full-on boot room or entranceway – as your own personal lobby. It's the first thing that your guests will see of your space, and, more importantly, it's also the greeting you receive when returning from a long day at work. This is the first opportunity to greet your senses with joy. Some ideas on that front include laying interesting tiles topped with rugs on the floors, fitting a crystal ceiling light, and hanging a series of joyful framed pictures of flowers, animals or something more modern, such as a poster of your favourite band, on the walls. What's behind the view of the space beyond your front door? Whether it's a staircase, a wall or an arch into a room, make it special with fairy lights, globe lights or exposed bulbs.

OPPOSITE The delectable interiors of Margate House Hotel offer interior inspiration at every turn, with a plaster-pink colour palette and carefully considered touches everywhere from the entrance hall to the bathrooms.

TANGO

HOST A

Grand Budapest Hotel

DINNER PARTY

Thanks to its focus on the pleasures of the body, *The Grand Budapest Hotel* provides plenty of suggestions for the food, drink and decoration needed to throw a themed shindig. Lashings of champagne should be obvious, and so should the main of olive-roasted duck. Delicate pastries are of great importance to any party indebted to the film, and if you can serve them in your own homemade Mendl's boxes then all the better.

Place names could come hanging in your new key board (instructions on how to make yours on page 202) in the form of tasselled keys with each guest's name and place number inscribed on it. The invitation could read as follows: 'Let it be known that the bearer of this document shall be permitted free and unmolested travel throughout my home. On the personal authority and decree of me, the host(ess) of this Zubrowkian luncheon.'

Suggested Dishes

MAIN
Duck roasted with olives

SIDES
Salad and champagne, darling

DESSERT
Pastries; a *religieuse* if you can get it

TABLESCAPE

A 1930s Zubrowkian luncheon would be a festival of finery, meaning you ought to bring out the fancy glassware and fine china that you keep for special occasions. Napkins should be either white linen or frilly and embroidered, and a vintage vase filled with peonies should be placed on one of the scalloped place mats that the serving dishes will sit on. Candles are always of the utmost importance at dinner parties, but for this theme they should come as tea lights in tulip-shaped holders.

PLAYLIST

— **Glenn Miller**, 'In the Mood'
— **Benny Goodman Sextet**, 'Moonglow'
— **Billie Holiday**, 'Strange Fruit'
— **Vera Lynn**, 'We'll Meet Again'
— **Fred Astaire**, 'Nice Work If You Can Get It'
— **The Ink Spots**, 'I Don't Want to Set the World on Fire'
— **Al Bowlly**, 'Heartaches'
— **Teddy Wilson**, 'Easy Living'
— **Fats Waller**, 'Ain't Misbehavin''
— **Art Tatum**, 'Tea for Two'

ZUBROWKIAN 31

Avoid having to drink the 'cat piss' they dole out in the Zubrowkian train dining car by serving Perrier Jouët champagne at your soirées. For a stiffer take on M. Gustave's favourite tipple, make it this mash-up of the pornstar martini and the French 75.

— 30ml (1US fl.oz) gin
— 15ml (½US fl.oz) passion fruit purée
— Chilled champagne

Mix the gin and purée in a glass, then top up with the champagne.

DREAM GUEST LIST

— César Ritz
— Stefan Zweig
— Lord Byron
— Otto Eckmann
— Alphonse Mucha
— Josephine Baker

HOW TO MAKE YOUR OWN KEY BOARD AND TASSELS

FOR THE KEY BOARD YOU WILL NEED

Materials

Pallet wood or other soft wood to cut to 340 x 215mm (13½ x 8½in)
220cm (90in) strip wood
Hooks
Red or pink paint

Tools

Claw hammer
Tape measure
Panel wood saw
Plate sander (60- and 120-grit sanding pads)
Pry bar
Wood glue
Drill
Pencil
Sash clamps
Mitre saw

TO MAKE THE KEY BOARD

1. If using a pallet, you will need to remove any nails to separate the slats using a claw hammer and pry bar, and cut so that when attached they will make a total size of 340 x 215mm (13½ x 8½in) using a panel wood saw. Sand the cut pieces to the required finish using 60-grit sandpaper followed by 120-grit.
2. Using wood glue, follow the manufacturer's instructions to join the slats together into one solid board. Secure using sash clamps.
3. Take a 9mm (⅓in) square strip of wood and joint the corners at 45 degrees to form a square, using a mitre saw. This will form the front edging.
4. Use wood glue to secure the strip wood to the front of the board.
5. Cut spacing strip wood to section the box into nine squares – you will need two pieces of wood the inside width of the box and a further six pieces of wood cut to equal size. Secure with wood glue and allow to dry.
6. Measure the mid-point of all nine sections and mark for hook holes.
7. Drill pilot holes and screw in the hooks (predrilling prevents splitting of wood).
8. Remove the hooks and paint the box in your chosen colour.
9. Allow the paint to dry, then replace the hooks.

FOR THE KEY TASSELS YOU WILL NEED

Materials

Card
Colourful yarn or embroidery thread
Keys and name tags
Slip rings

Tools

Scissors

TO MAKE THE KEY TASSELS

1. Cut the card to the length you want your tassels to be, and half of that length wide. For example, a 10cm (4in) tassel will require a 10 x 5cm (4 x 2in) piece of card.
2. Cut two pieces of yarn twice the desired length of your tassel and set aside.
3. Wrap the uncut length of yarn lengthways around the card, bearing in mind that the more you wrap, the thicker the finished tassel will be. Cut off the yarn when you have reached the desired thickness.
4. Holding this longer piece of yarn firmly at one end, use the scissors to cut it at the other end, then remove the card.
5. Open up the strands and tie one of the cut pieces around the middle of the bunch to create a knot.
6. Lift the bunch by the tied piece of yarn and fold in half.
7. Take the second strand of yarn and tie it around the bunch close to the top.
8. Trim the tassel to the desired length.
9. Repeat until you have enough tassels, then attach to keys and name tags using slip rings.

INDEX

INDEX OF DIY PROJECTS

Cottagecore Garland, How to Make 64–5
Countertop Mailbox, How to Make 132–4
Diner Condiment Box, How to Make 156–7
Ennui Crochet Coaster, How to Make 108–9
Gallery Wall, How to Create the Perfect 40
Key Box and Tassels, How to Make 202–3
Knitted Beanie Table Favours, How to Make 178–9
Skull and Crossbone Trinket Box, How to Make 86–7

GENERAL INDEX

1950s Americana 135–158

A
Adidas 26
Ahluwalia, Waris 70–71, 72
Ajrak 78
analogue 11, 58, 95, 97
Anderson, Eric 75
Anderson, Wes 6, 7, 8, 8, 9, 10, 10, 11, 12, 13, 14, 15, 17, 21, 24, 25, 26, 33, 45, 49, 50, 58, 61, 62, 69, 74, 75, 83, 91, 94, 95, 96, 97, 102, 103, 113, 116, 117, 118, 119, 124, 125, 126, 139, 142, 145, 149, 161, 164, 167, 168, 171, 176, 178, 183, 187, 188, 190, 192
animation 9
antiques (*see* 'vintage')
Art Deco 74, 81, 194, 197
Art Nouveau 186, 190, 191, 194, 195, 196, 197
Ash 11, 52, 61
Asteroid City (2023) 8, 9, 10, 11, 13, 15, 61, 135–158, 140–141, 142, 143, 144, 145, 152, 153
Atkins, Annie 188

B
Bandhani 78
bathroom 36, 153, 158–179, 198
Bean, Frank 58, 63
bedroom 61, 82, 128, 180–203
Belafonte 161, 164, 166, 172, 174, 177
Bengal Lancer, The 72, 73, 74,
Berensen, J K L 95, 95, 102
Bishop, Lionel 120
Bishop, Murray 120
Bishop, Rudy 120
Bishop, Suzy 13, 15, 116, 116, 117, 118, 119, 119, 122, 126
block printing 75, 78
Boggis, Walter 62
Bottle Rocket (feature length; 1996) 6, 8, 116
Bottle Rocket (short; 1993) 6
Brody, Adrien 69, 72, 72, 74, 82, 83
Bunce 62

C
Campbell, Midge 153
Canonero, Milena 144
Captain Hennessey 167
Captain Sharp 116, 119
Chalamet, Timothée 104
Chekhov, Anton 26
Clooney, George 9
colour 12, 13, 28, 30, 32, 34, 36, 54, 72, 74, 75, 76, 78, 85, 96, 98, 100, 103, 104, 105, 122, 128, 146, 149, 151, 152, 153, 168, 171, 183, 186, 192, 194, 197
  colour blocking 94
  colour drenching 11, 13, 30, 32, 83, 103, 187
  colour palette 25, 49, 73, 95, 117, 143, 165, 187
  colour wheel 11
  complementary colours 13, 83
  contrasting colours 13
Commander Pierce 119
Constable, John 48

Coppola, Roman 11, 117
cottagecore 9, 42¬–65, 128
Cousteau, Jacques 164, 165, 166, 167, 167, 170, 178
craftsmanship 11, 15, 45, 69, 74, 75, 81, 83, 118, 126, 188, 190

D

Dafoe, Willem 174, 175
Dahl, Roald 10, 45, 49, 50
Daimler, Klaus 174, 175
Darjeeling Limited, The (2007) 8, 10, 13, 15, 64–87, 70–71, 72, 74, 82, 83, 126, 142
Del Toro, Benicio 96
den 37, 124, 166
detail(s) 14, 15, 17, 25, 36, 72, 74, 116, 119, 170, 187
dining room 60, 83, 104, 135–158
dopamine decor 180–203
dried flowers 54, 56, 63, 65

E

Earp, Conrad 143, 144
Eckmann, Otto 195
European charm 88¬–109

F

Fantastic Mr. Fox (2009) 9, 10, 11, 13, 42–65, 46–47, 49, 52, 60, 61, 176
Fiennes, Ralph 50, 186, 186, 189
French Dispatch, The (2021) 9, 10, 88–109, 92–93, 94, 95, 96, 97, 104, 105, 124, 142
Friedberg, Mark 74, 166

G

gallery wall 10, 30, 40, 94, 102, 124, 149
Goldblum, Jeff 167
Grand Budapest Hotel, The (2014) 9, 10, 13, 75, 81, 105, 142, 176, 180–203, 184–185, 186, 187, 188, 189, 191
Guimard, Hector 188

H

hallway 13, 64¬–87, 175, 198
houseplants 30, 54, 56, 76, 98, 122, 146, 168, 192, 194, 197, 198
Howitzer Jr, Arthur 94, 98, 100, 105

I, J, K

interior design 7, 9, 11, 14, 17, 24, 33, 48, 75, 116, 183
Isle of Dogs (2018) 9, 10, 15
Johansson, Scarlett 140–141, 143, 152, 153
Kalamkari 78
Keitel, Harvey 119
kitchen 13, 42¬–65, 128, 151
kitsch 6, 7, 9, 17, 18¬–41, 76, 82
Klimt, Gustav 195

L

Leighton, Frederic 21
Lieutenant Nescaffier 106
Life Aquatic with Steve Zissou, The (2004) 8, 13, 153, 158–179, 162–163, 164, 165, 166, 174, 175
light fitting(s) 30, 33, 37, 76, 98, 122, 146, 168, 192, 194, 198
living room 13, 18¬–41, 105

M

M. Gustave 13, 186, 186, 189, 191, 191, 201
maximalism 11, 24, 72, 74, 75
mid-century modern 11, 17, 33, 82, 94, 104, 113, 117, 125, 139, 145, 151, 154, 188, 192
mid-twentieth century (see 'mid-century modern')
Miller, Arthur 26
mise en scene 9, 49, 142
Moonrise Kingdom (2012) 9, 10, 11, 15, 102, 110–135, 114–115, 116, 117, 118, 119, 120, 121
Moran, Kris 145
Mr Fox 48, 49, 50, 58
Mrs Fox 13, 48, 49, 49, 50, 58
Murray, Bill 36, 36, 92–93, 94, 95, 96, 105, 105, 120, 120, 162–163, 164, 165, 165, 174

N

nautical Mediterranean 158–179
nooks and crannies 110–135
Norton, Edward 61, 118, 119, 143
nostalgia 28, 117, 148, 161, 166

O, P

office 88¬–109, 174
Orient Express, The 74, 83
original features 27, 28
Paltrow, Gwynth 7, 22–23, 24, 36, 37, 166
patio 152
pattern 34, 72, 73, 75, 78, 81, 83, 96, 105, 125, 168, 186, 187, 194, 197
Phoenician Scheme, The (2025) 10
Pinnock, Anna 190
Pinter, Harold 26
Plimton, Ned 174, 175
Portman, Natalie 74
props 10, 30, 83, 97, 103, 117, 126, 188
  period props 11, 28, 49, 183, 188
puppetry 9, 10, 15, 188

R

Rajasthani Deco 64¬–87
retro 25, 54, 117
Rosenthaler, Moses 96
Royal Tenenbaums, The (2001) 6, 7, 7, 9, 11, 13, 18–41, 22–23, 24, 26, 27, 28, 36, 37, 73, 76, 94, 102, 124
Rushmore (1998) 8

S

Sam 116, 117, 119, 119, 120, 125
Sazerac, Herbsaint 91, 96, 97, 98, 102
Scalamandre 24, 25
Schwartzman, Jason 69, 72, 82, 83, 144, 153
Scout Master Ward 118, 119, 125
second-hand (see 'vintage')
set design 143
Shawshank Redemption, The (1994) 119
St Clair, Raleigh 36, 36, 38
Steenbeck, Augie 144, 153
Stiller, Ben 7, 26, 27
Stockhausen, Adam 10, 96, 145, 149, 190
Streep, Meryl 9
Swinton, Tilda 94, 95, 95
symmetry 6, 11, 30, 33, 98, 128, 183, 190

T

Tenenbaum, Chas 7, 25, 26, 27, 28
Tenenbaum, Etheline 7, 24, 26, 28, 28, 30, 32, 34, 36
Tenenbaum, Margot 7, 13, 22–23, 24, 24, 25, 26, 26, 28, 33, 36, 36, 37, 38
Tenenbaum, Richie 22–23, 25, 26, 28, 30, 32, 33, 34, 37, 37, 38, 39, 124
Tenenbaum, Royal 26, 34, 38
texture 58, 81, 82, 187, 194, 197
Tuttle, Charles H 27

V, W

vintage 17, 33, 34, 52, 54, 58, 60, 76, 98, 119, 126, 153, 168, 170, 171, 175
  vintage lighting 24, 54, 56, 85, 98, 122, 126, 146
wallpaper 24, 25, 50, 81, 117, 125, 126, 144, 149, 195, 197
whimsy 6, 9, 11, 78, 81, 83, 110–135, 145
Whitman, Francis 69, 75, 82, 83
Whitman, Jack 69, 76, 82, 83
Whitman, Peter 69, 82, 83
Wild West 144, 149
Willis, Bruce 116
Wilson, Owen 8, 69, 72, 82, 83, 91, 96, 97, 116, 166, 167, 175
Winchester, Sarah 21
Wonderful Story of Henry Sugar, The (2023) 10, 50
Wright, Jeffrey 96, 105
Wright, Roebuck 96, 102, 105, 106

Z

Zeffirelli 104
Zissou, Ned 167
Zissou, Steve 161, 164, 165, 167, 176

AUTHOR BIO

Jessie Atkinson is a writer and tastemaker from Manchester, UK, who has written extensively for magazines such as *British GQ* and *NME*. As a film obsessive and lover of home interiors, she has been a fan of Wes Anderson since she first watched *The Grand Budapest Hotel* in 2014. Her favourite films are *Isle of Dogs* and *The Royal Tenenbaums*, and she hopes that Wes will one day make a horror film.

ACKNOWLEDGEMENTS

All of the DIY projects in the book have been conceptualized and written by Alan Atkinson and Jane Atkinson. Our sincere thanks to them for this contribution.

The publisher would like to thank the following for supplying images.

41, 64–65, 87, 109, 133, 157, 179, 203 illustrations by Masako Kubo Illustration

2tl Pictorial Press Ltd / Alamy Stock Photo; 2tm Frenchie Cristogatin; 2tr Album / Alamy Stock Photo; 2ml Frenchie Cristogatin; 2m Cinematic / Alamy Stock Photo; 2mr Emma Jane Palin; 2bl Moviestore Collection Ltd / Alamy Stock Photo; 2bm Divine Savages; 2br Everett Collection Inc / Alamy Stock Photo; 4 Esther Maglitto @el_loves_colour; 7 Everett Collection Inc / Alamy Stock Photo; 8–9 Entertainment Pictures / Alamy Stock Photo; 10 Everett Collection Inc / Alamy Stock Photo; 12l Colours of Arley; 12r YesColours; 14(all) Hollis Loudon Interiors; 15(all) de Gournay; 16 Hollis Loudon Interiors; 18 ©Pure & Original / Margaret de Lange / Colour designer: Dagny Thurnmann-Moe KOI Colour Studio / Stylist: Kirsten Visdal / Walls, ceiling and doors in Old Ocre; 22–23 Pictorial Press Ltd / Alamy Stock Photo; 24 Moviestore Collection Ltd / Alamy Stock Photo; 25 Hollis Loudon Interiors; 26 United Archives GmbH / Alamy Stock Photo; 27 Maximum Film / Alamy Stock Photo; 28 Cinematic / Alamy Stock Photo; 29 Phaedra Brown @houseandgardendog; 31 Andreas von Einsiedel / Alamy Stock Photo; 32l YesColours; 32r Andreas von Einsiedel / Alamy Stock Photo; 34 Hollis Loudon Interiors; 35 Sarisa Munoz @indigoleopardhome; 36 Maximum Film / Alamy Stock Photo; 37 United Archives GmbH / Alamy Stock Photo; 42 Lisa Herr @herneutralcottage; 46–47 AJ Pics / Alamy Stock Photo; 48l Bambi Costanzo @number131; 48r Andreas von Einsiedel / Alamy Stock Photo; 49 AJ Pics / Alamy Stock Photo; 50 Renae Huffaker @HoningHuffAcres; 51 Liisi Väli; 52 Photo 12 / Alamy Stock Photo; 53 Elizabeth Whiting & Associates / Alamy Stock Photo; 55 Amy Whyte @amycwhyte; 57 Alexandra Wojtal @colorolii; 59 Sandra Baker @the_idle_hands; 60 Cinematic / Alamy Stock Photo; 61 Photo 12 / Alamy Stock Photo; 66 Sarisa Munoz @indigoleopardhome; 70–71 Moviestore Collection Ltd / Alamy Stock Photo; 72 Cinematic / Alamy Stock Photo; 73 Frenchie Cristogatin; 74 Moviestore Collection Ltd / Alamy Stock Photo; 77 India Holmes; 78 Sarisa Munoz @indigoleopardhome; 79 Divine Savages; 80 Frenchie Cristogatin; 81 Hollis Loudon Interiors; 82 Everett Collection Inc / Alamy Stock Photo; 83 Entertainment Pictures / Alamy Stock Photo; 88 Laura Karasinski / Atelier Karasinski; 92–93 Album / Alamy Stock Photo; 94 Photo 12 / Alamy Stock Photo; 95 Photo 12 / Alamy Stock Photo; 96 Album / Alamy Stock Photo; 97 TCD/Prod.DB / Alamy Stock Photo; 99 Laura Karasinski / Atelier Karasinski; 100 Andreas von Einsiedel / Alamy Stock Photo; 101 Andreas von Einsiedel / Alamy Stock Photo; 102l Laura Karasinski / Atelier Karasinski; 102r Emma Jane Palin; 103 Sarah Makant @JolliesandFollies; 104 Photo 12 / Alamy Stock Photo; 105 Everett Collection Inc / Alamy Stock Photo; 110 ALAMY; 114–115 Album / Alamy Stock Photo; 116 LANDMARK MEDIA / Alamy Stock Photo; 117 Cinematic / Alamy Stock Photo; 118 LANDMARK MEDIA / Alamy Stock Photo; 119 Album / Alamy Stock Photo; 120 LANDMARK MEDIA / Alamy Stock Photo; 121 Cinematic / Alamy Stock Photo; 123 Elizabeth Whiting & Associates / Alamy Stock Photo; 124l Liisi Väli; 124r Sandra Baker @the_idle_hands; 125 Amanda Cotton @houselust; 127tl Sandra Baker @the_idle_hands; 127tr Natasha James / Tasha Textiles; 127b Emma Jane Palin; 129 Andreas von Einsiedel / Alamy Stock Photo;

135t Andreas von Einsiedel / Alamy Stock Photo; 135bl Andreas von Einsiedel / Alamy Stock Photo; 135br Image Source Limited / Alamy Stock Photo; 136 Esther Maglitto @ el_loves_colour; 140–141 LANDMARK MEDIA / Alamy Stock Photo; 142 LANDMARK MEDIA / Alamy Stock Photo; 143 Album / Alamy Stock Photo; 144 Photo 12 / Alamy Stock Photo; 145 LANDMARK MEDIA / Alamy Stock Photo; 147 Frenchie Cristogatin; 148 Merve Kahraman; 149l Hana Snow @hana.snow; 149r Esther Maglitto @el_loves_colour; 150 Emma Jane Palin; 151 Andreas von Einsiedel / Alamy Stock Photo; 152 LANDMARK MEDIA / Alamy Stock Photo; 153 LANDMARK MEDIA / Alamy Stock Photo; 158 Emma Jane Palin; 162–163 Everett Collection Inc / Alamy Stock Photo; 164 Entertainment Pictures / Alamy Stock Photo; 165 Shutterstock.com; 166 Cinematic / Alamy Stock Photo; 167 Associated Press / Alamy Stock Photo; 169 Andreas von Einsiedel / Alamy Stock Photo; 170 Andreas von Einsiedel / Alamy Stock Photo; 171 Andreas von Einsiedel / Alamy Stock Photo; 172 Emma Jane Palin; 172–173 Anson Smart; 174 AJ Pics / Alamy Stock Photo; 175 Entertainment Pictures / Alamy Stock Photo; 180 Divine Savages; 184–185 Photo 12 / Alamy Stock Photo; 186 BFA / Alamy Stock Photo; 187 LANDMARK MEDIA / Alamy Stock Photo; 188 Cinematic / Alamy Stock Photo; 189 Album / Alamy Stock Photo; 190 dpa picture alliance / Alamy Stock Photo; 191 Pictorial Press Ltd / Alamy Stock Photo; 193 Hanna K L @hanna.k.l; 194 Andreas von Einsiedel / Alamy Stock Photo; 195l Esther Maglitto @el_loves_colour; 195r Sandra Baker @the_idle_hands; 196 Glasshouse images / Alamy Stock Photo; 197l Sandra Baker @the_idle_hands; 197r Divine Savages; 199(all) Margate House Hotel

Back cover images (clockwise, from top left):
Hanna K L @hanna.k.l; Laura Karasinski / Atelier Karasinski; ©Pure & Original / Margaret de Lange; Frenchie Cristogatin; Anson Smart; Amanda Cotton @Houselust; Sarah Makant @JolliesandFollies; Emma Jane Palin.

First published in Great Britain in 2025 by Greenfinch
An imprint of Quercus
Part of John Murray Group

A CIP catalogue record for this book is available from the British Library

HB ISBN 978-1-52944-719-4
EBOOK ISBN 978-1-52944-720-0

10 9 8 7 6 5 4 3

Illustrations by Masako Kubo
Cover design by Studio Polka
Printed and bound in China by C&C Offset Printing Co., Ltd.

Papers used by Quercus are from well-managed forests and other responsible sources.

Quercus
Carmelite House
50 Victoria Embankment
London EC4Y 0DZ

John Murray Group
Part of Hodder & Stoughton Limited
An Hachette UK company

The authorised representative in the EEA is Hachette Ireland, 8 Castlecourt Centre, Dublin 15, D15 XTP3, Ireland (email: info@hbgi.ie)